Life Lessons

By Nancy Blodgett Klein and Torrevieja Writers' Circle Members

LIFE LESSONS: GUIDANCE FOR ALL AGES

First edition. February 24, 2024.

ISBN: 979-8224774272

Written by Nancy Blodgett Klein.

For Alex, Andy and all young people
that they keep these life lessons in mind
all the days of their lives

Introduction
by Nancy Blodgett Klein

Why did I want to publish this book? As we live and have a variety of experiences, we learn and grow. Ideally, by the time we are in our sixties, we have learned many lessons about what works and what does not in terms of having a meaningful life. By this point in our lives, many of us want to share what we have learned with younger people so they can avoid the same mistakes and make better choices. So my original intent in this book was to pass along my own life lessons to younger generations, to share my wisdom gained from life experience.

But one of the life lessons I have learned is you cannot do it alone. We always need help from others to be successful in life. That's why I asked other members of the Torrevieja Writers' Circle (TWC) to also contribute. Like me, they are mature people, many of them retired expats, who also have wisdom to share with others. This kind and talented group of writers encouraged me to finish my previous book, *Torn Between Worlds: A Mexican immigrant's journey to find herself.* Without their encouragement and suggestions for improvements, my book would never have been published. That would have been a shame, too, as it has received many positive reviews. People who have read it said when they finished it, they were sorry it is over because they so enjoyed reading it.

Clearly, we need each other. That being the case, I knew that if other TWC members shared their own life lessons in this book it would make for a richer, more powerful experience for the reader. We hope you agree and that you find some wisdom here that will help you have a more meaningful life going forward, whatever your age. Remember each lesson is specific to the writer's life and you may not agree with all of them. That's okay, too. Happy reading!

Editor's note: For writers who are British or Canadian, the British spelling for words has been used, such as metre, rather than meter. For American writers, the American spelling of words has been used such as humor, rather than humour. At the same time, word usage has also been respected according to one's native country. For example, the word torch is used for British writers rather than substituting the American word flashlight.

ABOUT THE CONTRIBUTORS

All contributors are native English speakers and members of the Torrevieja Writers' Circle on the Costa Blanca in Spain. Several are British two are Canadian and two are from the US. We meet on a weekly basis (via Zoom or in person) to share our writing, critique each other's work and give each other encouragement and support in the writing craft.

Contributors to this Life Lessons Anthology include:

Sue Champion

Susan was educated mainly in Kenya, East Africa. At age seventeen she returned to her native England with her family and attended a catering college. A few years later, she returned to Kenya and worked in a beach resort. From there she travelled to South Africa and then Rhodesia, (now Zimbabwe), intending to continue working her way to Australia. However, that was where she met David, and from then on, they worked together, mainly in the hospitality industry. Susan began writing after retiring to Spain, where she joined the Torrevieja Writers' Circle, and discovered a love of writing, especially poetry. Her first book of poetry was published in 2017, entitled *Prayer, Praise and Poetry*. She lives on the Costa Blanca, in the Alicante province of Spain.

Geoff Cooper

Born in 1937, in industrial Tyneside, England, Geoff is a retired school teacher, head teacher, school inspector and now a writer. He lived most of his life in small town Northumberland in the north of England. He served in the Royal Air Force for two years, enjoying the privileges of travel: mainly to Cyprus, but also visiting Iraq, the Arabian Gulf States and Aden. He then attended St John's College, York and qualified as a teacher. All his teaching career was spent in Northumberland. At age thirty, he was head teacher of a tiny village primary school. Then for many years before retirement, he was head teacher of a large middle school. After that, he served with the school inspection service, *The Office for Standards in Education* (OfSTED), working full-time all-over England until the age of 71. He lives in the Alicante Province of Spain with his wife, Jeanie, a church minister. Geoff has three children, two of whom are headteachers in England. The other child escaped to the USA, where she manages a medical clinic in California.

Brenda Darling

Brenda was raised in the East End of London. She says she is "Cockney born and bred." In England, she worked as a support worker with adults with learning disabilities. She now lives on the Costa Blanca in Spain with her partner Derek. As a long-time member of the Torrevieja Writers Circle, he has found much inspiration and encouragement to achieve her ambition of publishing her own book.

S. Lee Follender

Lee is a consultant and author with expertise in communications, transformational studies, curriculum design, copywriting and training. She has served as Director of Management Training to major corporations and ghost writer for authors and individuals. Her experience has spanned multiple industries from high tech to beauty and government agencies to educational faculties. Her experience coaching entrepreneurs and individuals in looking for what purposeful action is next in their lives has brought her much joy and satisfaction. She lives in Austin, Texas, where she writes, paints, sculpts, and manages a lively coaching practice. She is author of *The Book of Being*.

John Edwards

John grew up in Herefordshire, a very rural county in England. That's where his roots still remain. Wildlife was all around and this created the interests that he still has to this day, such as birdwatching. He also enjoys writing poetry and short stories. He is a member of Stanza Mar Menor, San Miguel Writers and The Poetry Society in London. From 1964 to 1994, he was a police officer in The Metropolitan Police in London.

Darlene Foster

Darlene grew up on a ranch in Alberta, Canada, where her love of reading inspired her to see the world and write stories about a young girl who travels to interesting places in the Amanda Travels Series. Over the years she worked in rewarding jobs such as an employment counsellor, ESL teacher, recruiter, and retail manager, writing whenever she had a few spare minutes. She is now retired and has a house in Spain where she writes full time. When not travelling, meeting interesting people, and collecting ideas for her books, she enjoys spending time with her husband Paul and entertaining rescue dogs, Dot and Lia. https://www.darlenefoster.ca/

Anthony Jones

Anthony was born in Winchester, England in 1948. He was raised in Sussex, left for London and never went back, working for thirty years in graphic design and later on in education. Now living on the Costa Blanca with his wife Bobbie, he devotes his time to writing and is a contributor to *Boxing News*. His days are spent sipping martinis on his solarium while jotting down *bon mots* on this laptop.

Nancy Blodgett Klein

Nancy was a journalist and magazine editor in the Chicagoland area for many years. She has published hundreds of magazine articles on legal, social and political topics, including for the *American Bar Association Journal*. Later on, she was a public school teacher, including eight years teaching mostly Mexican bilingual students. She has masters' degrees in both Journalism and Education. Her first novel was published in 2021 and is titled *Torn Between Worlds: A Mexican Immigrant's journey to find herself.* She also writes a blog called spainwriter.home.blog covering a wide variety of topics. She now lives in Orihuela Costa, in the Alicante province of Spain, with her husband Rick.

John McGilvray

John has lived in Torrevieja, Spain, for twenty years and have been a member of San Miguel Writers for seven or eight years. He writes mostly poetry and has had several poems published in various anthologies. His interests are badminton, running, chess and reading. He has competed in two London Marathons including the very first one in 1981. He lives with his partner Carole in Spain.

Maureen Moss

Maureen lives in a small seaside town called La Mata, near Torrevieja, in the Alicante province of Spain. Before becoming a Tour Leader/Guide, she was a personnel consultant, languages teacher, travel agent, management trainer, travel writer, and a book publisher, in roughly that order. Also, throughout her early career, she frequently organized and led group and family tours in Europe. She has a consultancy business specializing in training tour guides and DMCs, including communication and management skills. She loves learning languages and speaks six foreign languages, to varying levels. In her spare time, she loves walking her dogs on the beach, listening to world music, and trying to learn Spanish dances. She loves reading and writing about travel and she is a published author.

Val Peachey, PH.D

As an experienced educator, Valerie brings over 25 years of expertise in the higher education sector in Canada and Australia. Having been at the forefront of online learning, she has led several successful institutional initiatives in the digital and open environment, creating access for stakeholders both in the corporate and educational arenas. As a highly respected leader, she believes that open pathways, flexible and well-designed learning opportunities, can yield transformative results. Individuals gain increased opportunities to reach their personal and professional goals, unhindered by geographical or time constraints. Often recognised by colleagues for her enthusiasm, energy and tenacity Valerie is often called upon to share her insights at conferences and professional gatherings. Valerie's passion lies in helping others fulfil their potential, which she has gathered from a lifetime of experiences.

Andrea Peers

Born and educated in Yorkshire, England, Andrea started her working life as a Civil Servant in the Ministry of Defence. Later, as a mature student, she studied fashion design at Harrogate College of Art and Design and then began designing and making wedding dresses. Some years later she had another business, supplying coffee to hotels and restaurants, before moving to Spain, where she and her husband formed a company offering a property finding service and made lifelong friends of different nationalities. She now enjoys retired life in an English village.

Table of Contents

29. There is something special about the Irish
30. Don't judge a book by its cover
31. Famous relatives can inspire you
32. Be grateful for little things, especially when life isn't going well
33. Don't play favorites with your children
34. A loving relationship can make life's last stage more enjoyable

Make a Difference By Helping Others
By Nancy Blodgett Klein

"My religion is quite simple. My religion is kindness."— *Dalai Lama XIV*

When I was in my thirties, I worked as an editor for a legal management magazine. One day while at work, I had one of my co-workers, a petite blonde woman in her late twenties who I will call Sheila, review an article I intended to publish in the legal management association publication. I had Sheila review the article because it concerned an area of the association where she worked and thought getting her input might be a good idea. After she returned it to me, it had many changes and questions. This I did not like. I was angry that she hadn't simply approved it with minor or no changes. Obviously, I had issues of my own, such as too much pride in my work product. For many months after this, I decided to not even talk to Sheila when I passed her in the hallway of the association offices. In time, I discovered this young woman was married, like me, but was unable to have any children. She really wanted children and decided to try adopting a child.

To do this, though, she had to effectively compete for the attention and interest of the pregnant mothers-to-be. She had to know how to say the right things to get the mother of the child to be adopted interested in considering her and her husband as adoptive parents. At the time, I had just given birth to our first son Alex and spend part of my maternity leave reading the *Seven Habits of Highly Effective People*. One of the habits that really resonated with me was to "Begin with the End in Mind" when living your life. Best-selling author Stephen Covey advises readers to think about how you want to be remembered at your funeral or memorial service. Visualize your loved ones on that day. What will they say about you?

"What character would you like them to have seen in you? What contributions, what achievements would you want them to remember?

Look carefully at the people around you. What difference would you like to have made in their lives?"

The idea of beginning with the end in mind had a profound effect on me. I knew now I wanted to be remembered as a kind, compassionate person who had made a positive difference in the lives of others. This key idea from the *Seven Habits* changed me so much that when I returned to work from my maternity leave, I wanted to help Sheila.

I asked her if she wanted me to help her write a letter that would get a pregnant woman interested in meeting with her and her husband. Up to this point, the letter they had written had gotten them zero meetings with the mothers-to-be. Sheila said, "Yes, please. We need help." After that, she showed me a book of letters people had written to get the interest of the pregnant women, including their letter. Through reviewing this book, I was able to see which letters were effective with their messages and which were not.

"Why do you want a child?" I asked Sheila. "Why would you and your husband be the best couple to raise someone else's child?" I explained to her that what was most important was to stand out from the others, getting the mother's attention about why they were the best option. They had to market themselves better, in effect, to get a child. Keeping this in mind, I helped Sheila write a letter that was successful in getting her a meeting with a pregnant mother. Ultimately, this meeting led to her and her husband adopting a child.

Now that I am getting closer to the end of my life, I look back on this experience as one time I made a positive difference to someone else. Rather than holding onto anger about something trivial, I decided to be compassionate instead and open my heart to Sheila, helping her and her husband adopt a much-desired child.

Life Lesson: Always be kind and helpful. By doing this, you can make a big difference in other peoples' lives and in your own.

Try to Find Good in Everyone
By Darlene Foster

"A stranger is just a friend you haven't met yet." – Will Rogers

How do we find our friends? Let's face it, they were all strangers initially. Friends come in all shapes and sizes. It would be very boring if all of our friends were the same. I've made friends through work, special interest groups, places of worship, social functions and travelling. Through friends of friends, through my children and even when dog walking. If you think about your good friends, remember how you first met and how the friendship developed. Did you hit it off immediately or did it take time to get to know each other? Maybe you didn't even care for each other until you found something in common.

My father always said you can find something in common with everyone you meet, and if you look hard enough, you will find something good in everyone. I have found that to be true in many instances. When I first meet someone I don't find that pleasant or who rubs me the wrong way, instead of walking away, I consider it a challenge. Anyone can befriend a likeable, easy-going person. But, everyone has a story, and if you get to know a person, you can always find something in common or something likeable.

As a child, I would befriend the person sitting in the corner, all alone. Later, as a teenager, I risked being shut out of the in-crowd by chatting to the mixed-race girl everyone else was being mean to.

My first job was working in a gift shop in a small prairie city where one regular customer always came in grouchy and demanding. No one wanted to wait on her. When she entered the store everyone rolled their eyes. As the youngest and newest member of staff, I was sent out to help her. I always smiled at her, even though she didn't smile back, and was attentive to her needs. I helped her find the perfect gift for an elderly aunt and the right colour candles and placemats for her dining room table. One day I complimented her on a vintage brooch she was wearing. I caught a glimmer of a smile as she told me it had belonged to her mother. I continued to be nice to her whenever she came into the store and always asked about her family and her health. She spent a lot of money in the store and my boss was pleased. This woman started to ask for me whenever she came into the store. When her first grandson was born, she was excited and eagerly shared his picture with me.

During that time period, the local radio station held a contest for best salesclerk in town. People sent in explanations for why they thought a particular salesperson should win the prize. I didn't win first prize, but I got some votes and one was from this difficult customer. Someone from the radio station dropped off the letters and hers was glowing. I found out later most of her Jewish family had died in Germany during the Holocaust. She probably had trouble trusting anyone. It was a good lesson for me.

Life lesson: You never know the burdens another person is carrying. Give everyone a chance. The first impression is not always the real person. Like all relationships, friendship takes work, understanding and empathy. Treat everyone with respect, they may become a good friend one day. As Maya Angelou once observed, "People will forget what you said, people will forget what you did, but people will never forget how you made them feel."

Sometimes It's Best to Just Look Away
By Nancy Blodgett Klein

"Whatever is true, whatever is noble, whatever is right, whatever is pure, whatever is lovely, whatever is admirable—if anything is excellent or praiseworthy—think about such things."
—The Bible, Philippians 4:8

My first job after graduating from Journalism School in 1979 was working as a police reporter in the City of Chicago. To find stories, I was required to go to different police stations around the city to see what I could learn about the day's mayhem. We were supposed to cover the worst things that could happen, like murder, big fires, major car crashes, train wrecks and other tragedies.

I figured out very quickly that the police liked to kid around with the young reporters and they typically had a black sense of humor. For example, one police officer showed me a colored photo of a dead man whose face was covered with vomit. The cop was joking about how it looked like the dead man had eaten pepperoni pizza before he died.

On Friday, May 25' at the end of my first week on the job, when a police officer at the Rodgers Park police station pointed out smoke to me some miles west of the station and said it was coming from a plane that had crashed at O'Hare airport, I thought he was kidding. When I realized he was not, I then remembered that my parents were at the airport at that very moment, on their way to Florida.

So I called the city desk in a panic and asked, "Where was the plane that crashed headed?" The editor told me Los Angeles. So I breathed a sigh of relief and asked him what had happened with the plane that crashed. He said it was an American Airlines Flight 191 on its way to Los Angeles that had crashed just after takeoff when the left engine fell off the wing. Just unbelievable.

When the plane crashed in a field in Des Plaines, about 1,400 meters (4,600 feet) from the end of the runway, it burst into flames. Firefighters and police went to the area to see if there were any people that might have survived. What they saw and smelled instead were smoldering body parts. No one survived. The crash killed 258 passengers, 13 crew, plus two people on the ground. It was the deadliest plane crash ever in the United States.

One of my coworkers at the City News Bureau wire service where I worked could have passed for a policeman, with short black hair, conservative dress and a serious demeanor. Jerry was one of the first reporters to arrive at the scene of the crash. He told me while out for drinks at a bar after work that he went out on the smoky field where body parts were mixed among pieces of metal and broken cables. "Wow," I said, impressed that he got passed the police who typically block access to such scenes of carnage. "That must have been something to see." Jerry nodded, sipped his beer, and was quiet for a moment. Then he said, "I wish I hadn't gone. I saw burning flesh, smashed-up suitcases, and other things that I can't get out of my head now." I had not thought of this. Sometimes you want to rush into a situation to get a scoop but then you are unable to ever forget what you saw. It remains with you always, despite your efforts to block it out.

I continued to work for the City News Bureau, a wire service that supplied the *Chicago Tribune*, *Chicago Sun Times*, CBS, ABC, NBC and other television and radio stations with news, for another year. But seeing and reporting about death and destruction every weekday for a year really took its toll on me. I would frequently wake up in the middle of the night, drenched in sweat, from a nightmare I had just had.

Even so, I was curious about the death of some of the people I reported about. For example, for several months, I worked on the night shift, covering news events from 4 pm until midnight. On this shift, I got friendly with a staff member who worked at the Cook County Morgue. Bodies were sent there when people died from unnatural causes, such as through being beaten to death, shot or being killed in a car crash.

Once, during the night shift, I wrote a story about a teenage boy who had been killed in a car accident. I was talking to the staff worker at the morgue to get details about the victim, such as his name, where he lived, his age, and anything else he could tell me. The worker, David, told me the body was already there now. I asked him if I could come over and see it. He said sure.

I drove over and David said the body was in the basement in one of the coolers. I can't tell you why I wanted to see this particular body. By then, I had written about so many dead people. Maybe I just wanted to put a face with the name, for once. We went downstairs and he opened up a cooler that held at least six bodies. They were stacked on cots that were attached to the wall, with 3 cots on the left hand side of the cooler and three on the right. All the cots had bodies on them. David said, "Here is the boy you wrote your story about." I looked at his face and his eyes were closed. He could have been sleeping! The rest of his body looked undamaged. I said, "Thanks, David. I appreciate it." I didn't look at the other people, except to note that the rest of them looked a lot older.

I was ready to go back upstairs then, having made a connection to one of the people I had written about. Now I just felt sorry for his family. But David said, "Hey, do you want to see some Gacy victims? They are locked up in this cooler over here."

John Wayne Gacy Jr. was a Chicago area-based serial killer. He murdered at least 33 teenage boys and young men between 1972 and 1978 after sexually assaulting them. Gacy had buried 26 of his victims in the basement of his home. This was 1979, only a year after his crimes were uncovered and before many victims had been identified.

I thought it over for a few seconds and decided I didn't want to have these bodies stuck in my mind for the rest of my life and suffer the fate that happened to Jerry (and undoubtedly to the first responders) after seeing the remains of victims from the American Airlines crash at

O'Hare Airport. I decided it was best to not look at all because then I couldn't keep these images from haunting me for years to come.

Life Lesson: Sometimes it is best to avoid looking at what you don't really want to see. If you have a choice in the matter, look away and instead focus your mind on what is true, noble, right and pure.

Life Lesson: An Obsession with Money Can Make You Miserable

By Geoff Cooper

For the love of money is the root of all evil.—1 Timothy 6:10

It was like a lament. A slow, sad tune, played over and over again on wailing Scottish bagpipes. A haunting refrain. It was repeated over and over to whoever would listen. Not many chose to listen voluntarily. "I'm a prisoner in my own home," my Aunt Bessie would say, with a despairing wail. "I'm a prisoner in my own home," she would repeat. And, ultimately, it was true.

Aunt Bessie had said this to Jack, her former gardener, until he got sick of hearing it and wasn't ever coming again. She said it to the doctor who smiled gently at her, knowing there was nothing he or medical science could do, as he prescribed more pills.

"I'm a prisoner in my own home," she had said to her niece before they quarreled about the car her niece was driving. It had been made in Japan which she didn't approve of. "Aren't good cars made in England?" she had demanded. There were no more chances to say, "I'm a prisoner in my own home," to her niece because her niece stopped visiting her after that.

When I visited her in her old, cold cottage, where no improvements were even considered, Aunt Bessie always complained, "Things are so expensive these days," or she would whine, "I'm not saving as much as I used to." At each visit, she wore the same brown dress or her grey one. Never a different pair of shoes. "These are comfortable and will last," she would say. They did last, even when her feet were no longer able to walk in them. Someone called the place where she lived, 'Cold Comfort Farm.' And there was cold comfort there. I often asked her, "Why don't you do something for yourself?" "There isn't enough. I must save," she would reply.

Because my aunt had lots of money, a bank representative came to visit her to advise her how to invest her money better. "I'm a prisoner in my own home," she complained to the employee when he arrived. He looked around at the chipped and faded paintwork, the primitive kitchen, the torn cushions on her uncomfortable chairs and the gloomy heavy curtains, ripped to shreds by her cats. He knew why there was plenty of money in the bank. She was a miser, he thought, but he didn't say that. She was a good customer because she put money in the bank and withdrew little.

"She's a miser," the bank employee told his manager when he returned from the visit. Her bank manager knew her accountant and told him the story of the old woman, who had lots of money, was crippled, and unable to get out of her house but who kept on saving money. The accountant asked, have you been told, "'I'm a prisoner in my own home?" Their eyes met in recognition over their whisky glasses. The accountant recognized the story of my Aunt Bessie, the crone who paid her accountancy bill promptly every year. He knew it was just about the only bill she paid because she never bought anything. He had heard, "I'm a prisoner in my own home," twice a year for longer than he cared to remember when he visited there to do her accounts.

There had been a time, after her husband died, that her solicitor had said, "You could afford a Rolls Royce, if you wanted." She had only asked him if she could afford a new car. This was before she started saying, "I'm a prisoner in my own home," long before rheumatoid arthritis began to claim ownership of her body. She hadn't known who else to ask about buying a new car. She couldn't ask the new gardener. She couldn't ask the vicar who came to visit her from time to time. He would have wanted them to pray about it and she didn't feel comfortable praying about things like that. She only prayed that her shares paid dividends and didn't sustain any losses.

She would have like to have asked her children about whether she should buy a new car but she had none. She and her husband had tried hard. They'd seen doctors, had hospital investigations, but there was never a pregnancy. They had tried to adopt her brother-in-law's daughter but that didn't work out either.

Her new gardener, named Joe, had told her about the Mediterranean cruise he and his wife were saving up for. 'Waste of money', she thought. Silly waste of money when they could be buying shares in the company that has made her car, or in that petrol company she had shares in, or in that lovely clothing company that had made the dress she had bought years ago that she still wore.

Now Bessie was trapped. Plenty of money in the bank. She really could afford a Rolls Royce. That would have been good if she could still drive. She could afford - no, not a silly little seven-day Mediterranean cruise - but a world cruise. She would have enjoyed a world cruise. There were interesting things in the world to see. She saw them on the news on the old black-and-white television set she had that still worked well. No need to change that.

In time, moving about in her home became exceedingly difficult. But she did have a choice to make now. She hated the pills she was supposed to take. They made her feel worse, she was sure. Plus, there was no drink on the tray in front of her. So, really, there was no choice at all. She couldn't take pills without a drink to wash them down. She would have to tell the home help later when she came to put her to bed. The home help would have to be told off. The home help was careless and negligent. She couldn't understand how anyone could be careless and negligent. She had never been careless and negligent in her life and look at her now. She just couldn't take the pills, just as she couldn't drive a new Rolls Royce or go on a cruise around the world. Nor could she - nor would she - withdraw money from the bank once it had gone in. How poor I am, she thought. No children, no friends, no visitors, not even that praying vicar. A prisoner in my own home. All I have is money.

Life Lesson: Money is nice, as long as there is enough to go around. It is good to be able to earn money. Money can help

individuals to experience exciting events. But money cannot buy good health. Money does not buy life-long friendships or positive relationships. The only value money has is in what it can do for you and your loved ones.

Be the Change You Wish to See in the World
By Lee Follender

"Every human being's deepest, most natural expression is the desire to make a difference in life, of wanting to matter. We can choose to make the success of all humanity our personal business. We can choose to be audacious enough to take responsibility for the entire human family, to make our love for each other and for the world what our lives are really about."—Werner Erhard

As I lay awake the other night, after hearing the news and listening to a Korean friend speak with me regarding an article in the *New York Times* about recent murders in Minneapolis, I tossed and turned, wanting to sleep, yet experiencing enormous stress because of the troubled thoughts in my head.

How have we come to this; I asked myself. So much anger, hatred for others who are different and where will it end? What happened to the America I grew up in – trusted as "good and fair," home of the brave, stalworth defender of the poor and downtrodden? It all seems so far away right now – and yet, I continue to think of myself as an optimist; someone who believes that life is good – that Americans are kind. I believe we should care for each and every citizen – that we are a nation of immigrants, always striving to better ourselves and grow our communities into rich tapestries of different colors, different ethnicities and beliefs – all woven together in humanity's dream of a world that works for everyone – with no one left out.

We walked on the moon, didn't we? We defend the weak and support the poor, don't we? We are a nation of pilgrims – warriors for good; at least that is what I always thought as a girl, growing up in America. What has become of us – and what will our future hold?

As I lay thinking about all of that, my mind wandered back to a simpler time – to my youth, when I believed in that American dream and all that was possible for everyone in this, the promised land. Yet now, I am fearful that perhaps that wonderful dream was – and will never again be - real. Not for me – and not for generations to come. What will it take, I wonder, to bring what really matters back into focus? What will it take to eradicate the hatred, the need for citizens to arm themselves, for teachers to drill students on how to keep safe from an active shooter? How do we get rid of all the anger and the hate of those who are different from us? How can we end the suffering of people in poverty? And finally, how can we educate the ignorant to live differently?

How long will we be distanced – not only from each other because of disease – but from those halcyon days of my childhood? Did they ever really exist?

Evidently, only in my delusional, white majority world. Was I blind or just deluded? Were we ever really united in brotherhood, in citizenship, in democracy? I hunger to once again live in that fantasy world where everyone was free, equal and loved. I want to live again in my childhood dream, in these days.

I leave you with the following poem.

These Days...

Good or bad, wrong or right - Walk away or turn and fight?

Nothing's ever black and white.

These days...

Pick up a gun or put it down – Stay at home or go to town.

Wear a mask or just a frown.

These days...

Five years ago, who heard of Zoom – except a lens on a camera's boom-

And certainly not to avoid the gloom – of death.

These days...

We walked around with our nose in a book – still able to see a loving look,

Yet today we are stuck in a Kindle or Nook (or a phone or a tablet).

These days...

And hardly a day or week went by - when we'd have occasion to laugh or cry.

But now we're all fearful - and wondering why.

These days...

Computers are plenty but hugs are few – masks, gloves, and barriers between me and you,

And what news is false and what news is true?

These days...

A simpler time it seems has gone – Complexity tells us to keep moving on;

Don't worry about hugs – just wear masks when you run.

These days...

It's likely to pass and then we'll be free – to see old friends – to giggle with glee;

But who will be left - and will it be me?

These days...

It seems carefree times from the past may be done – whether through a bomb, a flood or the sun-

What will do us in – maybe a gun?

These days...

We've come so far – to the moon and back – yet it seems that love and compassion we lack;

Replaced with a hatred of anyone Asian or Black

These days...

Yes, the world's on our desktop, of that it is clear – We can Zoom cross the globe and see millions so clear,

Yet hate people not like us and have COVID to fear

These days...

And so my friends, it's easy to see that times have changed - and freedom's not free;

And now it is up you and to me.

These days...

Can we take up the cause for humanity's sake – Can we live with compassion rather than hate?

Will we stand up for justice or is it too late?

These days...

Life Lesson: During these troubled times, it's more important than ever that we be kind and caring, that we stand up peacefully for what Democracy can and should be. As global citizens, as human beings, we need to "choose to be audacious enough to take responsibility for the entire human family, to make our love for each other and for the world what our lives are really about."

Some Questions Don't Have Answers
By Nancy Blodgett Klein

"Zen wants us to acquire an entirely new point of view to look into the mysteries of life. This is because Zen has come to the definite conclusion that the ordinary logical process of reasoning is powerless to give final satisfaction to our deepest spiritual needs."—D.T. Suzuki

Are you an orphan? Are both your parents gone now? How do we deal with this? I think of both my mother and my father every day. Even though I had issues with them both growing up, now that they are gone, I feel their absence keenly. And I wonder will there ever be a day where I don't think of them or miss their loving acceptance of me? No one cares as much about you as your mother and father! That is, if you were lucky enough to have such a parent.

I had a very good friend I will call Alice who didn't have that kind of loving experience. She didn't feel loved growing up in the way I did because her mother was bipolar and was hospitalized several times when my friend Alice was a child. When her mother was home, she wasn't loving or particularly kind. In fact, she had few memories of her childhood. That, in itself, should have been a source of concern for me.

However, I didn't think too much about the traumatic upbringing that 57-year-old Alice had. I only knew that she was a great friend to be with. She was smart, funny, kind and interested in books, music and singing, as I was. We both had husbands who worked in Information Technology (they were also friends) and both of us had two children around the same ages. We were neighbors and attended the same church, singing in the alto section in the choir.

One fateful day, I talked to her on the phone and she told me she was depressed. I mistakenly thought I understood this feeling and said I was depressed too, when my mother died. Alice said, "No, what you felt was grief. Depression is different." She added that she felt like her life was over. Rather than ask her to go more deeply into her feelings of profound pain, I instead said, "You are just going through a transition," as one of her daughters was recently married and the other was planning to get married one year later. In retrospect, I wish I had just listened to her and not tried to talk her out of her feelings. This wasn't helpful. I also wanted to tell her I loved her but I didn't do that either. That was the last time I ever talked to Alice.

The following week, her husband called and told me Alice had taken her life in the bedroom of their shared suburban home. This was the most traumatic thing that had ever happened to me. Like others shaken by the suicide of a loved one, I could not make sense of what she had done. Why? Why? Why? This question just kept banging around in my head. I was hurt and angry. I wanted to confront her with my anger.

- Alice, why didn't you call me and tell me *explicitly* that you didn't want to live anymore? Maybe I could have said the right thing to save you. You didn't give me that chance.
- Did you think of your husband at all and how traumatic it would be for him to find you like that? He had to call 911 while trying to revive you. Jesus Christ.
- Did you think of your daughters and how hurt they would be, not just in the weeks or months or years that passed, but really for the rest of their lives? No mother to call when they give birth for the first time and had questions about what to do. No mother to share their amazing bundle of joy with. This absence will be profoundly felt, especially then, and on other special occasions that are too numerous to list.

I am glad you found a way to end your pain but for the survivors, for those of us who loved you, the pain just goes on and on. The pain goes on, the hurt goes on, and the anger goes on, in an endless alternating dance of troublesome, upsetting, emotions.

Suicide is just another word for murder. And you murdered my best friend. How could you do that? I am sorry but I don't feel understanding right now. Your death was a huge blow. And that makes me so angry at you. It didn't have to happen.

On other days, though, I yearn to forgive you. On such a day, I take a Zumba class because you told me it was fun to dance for exercise. I remember then what a good friend you were to me. We laughed a lot together and shared our joys, our sorrows, our otherwise unspoken hurts.

Some days I am so weary of life's demands that I don't want to go on either and that's when I feel some understanding of what you did. But most of the time, life is worth living. I am not going to blame you. But I am not going to feel guilt either. If you wanted to die, that was ultimately your choice. And I have to accept that I will never really understand why you took your life, even though you wrote not one, but two, suicide notes to explain your reasons. Some questions simply don't have adequate answers to satisfy our need for understanding.

Life Lesson: The suicide of a loved one really hurts. It's okay to be hurt and angry. It's okay to not really understand why. These feelings might never go away either. But don't blame yourself if someone you love has taken his/her life. It was truly out of your control.

Connect to the Sacred
By Nancy Blodgett Klein

"Do not dwell in the past, do not dream of the future, concentrate the mind on the present moment." — Buddha

The first time I looked death in the face I was 7 years old. I saw my beloved grandfather Charles in an open coffin. He had a red bruise on his forehead because he had fallen against the sink in the bathroom of his house in Chicago and hit his head when he had a heart attack. I was terribly upset about the red bruise on his forehead. That was almost more upsetting to me than his motionless body. He might be sleeping in the casket, but he shouldn't have a bright red bruise on his forehead.

That night at home, after the funeral, I asked my mother when she tucked me in bed, "What happens to people when they die?" She said that though a person's body may die, his or her soul lives on. I liked that answer. It made sense to me then and it still does today. When we die, I think we all go to heaven and meet up with God. I think everything that is mysterious to us now, such as why loved ones commit suicide, will be clear to us then. Or if it's not clear, at least it won't upset us anymore. I also believe that we were originally with God and that is why we long to be with him/her again. Our souls are connected to God and we yearn to be closer to this primal force in a place where we felt at home.

One way I feel most connected to God is through singing sacred music because it expresses the inexpressible. In particular, it beautifully expresses our longing for God. For example, one song written by Italian composer Giovanni Palestrina, *Sicut Cervus*, includes the words, "As a heart longs for the flowing streams, so longs my soul for thee, O God." On the web, it said this piece of music is considered to be "one of the great musical masterpieces of the Church and by many accounts the most outstanding example of religious choral art from the Renaissance."

Now people don't usually go around talking about their longing for God, but it is socially acceptable to express this desire in song. There is much more freedom of expression possible with music. In addition, through music your ego goes away. You aren't busy thinking about the past or future. You are very much in the moment. And being in the moment is where God can be found.

As spiritual guru and bestselling author Eckhart Tolle writes in *A New Earth, Awakening to Your Live's Purpose,* when we are thinking about the past or future, we are not really living our life. We are no longer in the present moment and that's the most important place to be. As Tolle writes, "Time isn't precious at all because it is an illusion. What you perceive as precious is not time but the one point that is out of time: the Now. That is precious indeed. The more you are focused on time — past and future — the more you miss the Now, the most precious thing there is."

Being in our ego, or stuck in our head preoccupied about something, rather than being where we are now and with who we are now keeps us from truly enjoying our life. When we are stuck in our ego, we are always somewhere else rather than in the here and now.

When I was still working full-time and raising two children, I was always thinking about what I had to do next. Life was just an endless series of tasks to complete. This was a stressful way to live and it made it hard to relax and enjoy the moment when you are always thinking about what you had to do later that day or what you would like to do on the weekend.

One activity that really helps to stop the incessant ego chatter is singing. If you don't have the voice for it, I also recommend meditating, stopping to appreciate beauty in art or nature, and any other acts that are about being, rather than doing. By being in the moment we can better connect to the place where God resides.

I realize this can be hard to do, of course. For example, I have a friend who I take yoga with who says she cannot stop thinking when she tries to meditate. "What are you thinking about when you meditate?" I asked her. "Nothing important, just things like what I need to buy at the supermarket later today." Does this sound like you? If so, remember that learning to meditate and be in the moment takes time and practice. But you can do this if you decide it is important enough to you.

Life Lessons: Being in the moment, rather than focusing on events in the past or on what might happen in the future, is a good way to connect with the beauty, the wonder and the sacredness of the world. Stop looking at your phone. Just slow down and appreciate life. Listen to the bird that sings in the tree, stop to look at the beautiful sunset. Appreciate the beauty of the stone you found on the street. Eat mindfully. Breathe slowly and deeply, with the intent of calming down your mind. Meditate. Do yoga. And of course, there is nothing like singing to focus yourself on the present moment.

Live Each Day as If It Were Your Last

By Susan Champion

"But about that day or hour no one knows, not even the angels in heaven, nor the Son, but only the Father.

Be on guard! Be alert! For you do not know when that time will come."
Mark 13: 32-33

It was a perfectly normal Sunday on the 4th of September 2011 in Spain. My husband's youngest daughter always phoned Sunday mornings. When she hadn't rung by the usual time, David seemed agitated and decided to phone her.

When his daughter asked him, "How are you today" He responded, "Fine. It is a lovely day, and I am taking my wife to the beach." This outing was news to me, and a nice surprise, as my husband was not a "beach" person.

Sure enough, having finished our coffee, we loaded the car for a beach day: chairs, beach umbrella, towels, books, snacks, etc. We wore shorts and t-shirts over our swimwear ready for the sea. Before we set off, David asked if I had other shoes, apart from flip flops, in case I should have to drive home. I laughed that off and said, "No. I know you prefer to drive."

The beach was crowded that day, but we found a spot for ourselves, and set up our chairs and brolly. We had been advised not to leave our stuff unattended, so we took turns swimming in the Mediterranean Sea. I went first. I love swimming in the sea when it is warm, and felt contented as I floated, gazing up at the sky.

Eventually, I reluctantly returned to our spot on the beach. It was David's turn. He had been reading. He took off his reading glasses and said, "Look after my glasses." I said, "Sure." Then I advised him to "go further down the beach where it is sandy because it's very stony here." And off he went.

I watched him walk away, but soon couldn't distinguish him among the masses of other people. I got out my book but couldn't concentrate for some reason. After about ten minutes, I wondered where he was. I knew he wouldn't stay in the water long. David was not a great swimmer. For some reason I felt anxious, and decided to risk abandoning our stuff, and started to walk slowly down the beach. I soon saw a crowd of people and started to panic. I just somehow knew there was something wrong. When I reached the crowd and pushed through, David was lying on the beach with a group of paramedics giving him CPR.

There was also a policeman there and I told him that this man was my husband, "Este hombre es mi marido." I think he told me to keep calm and let the medics do their job. I thought, he must have collapsed, and he'll be all right in a moment. But he wasn't. After what seemed like half an hour, but could have been ten minutes or two hours, they gave up. A woman standing next to me said "el esta muerto". I couldn't speak, so she said in English, "Do you understand?" I had understood the Spanish, but not the reality, so I shook my head. She said in English, "He is dead." I don't remember what I said, if anything, as I was in shock.

The kindly Spanish policeman was trying to ask me if I had a relative to call. David's brother and his wife lived in Campoverde, the same village as us, but I couldn't remember their phone number. (I didn't have a smart phone in those days). I managed to remember their address, and this policeman said he would go to their house, after helping me put all our stuff in our car. I got dressed over my bikini and went back to find people still on the beach, but the crowd had thinned out. The drama was over, although my dead husband was still lying there on the beach.

I believe God sends us angels, disguised as people, when we need them. I know that is what he did that day. Two English ladies appeared at my side. One asked me, "Are you English?" "Yes," I replied. Then they asked me if I was alone? "Yes," I answered. Then these angels in disguise said, "Well, you are not alone anymore. We are going to stay with you as long as necessary." One of the two ladies went to speak with the paramedics. When she came back, she explained she wanted to ensure she understood everything correctly before explaining it to me. She said that because my husband had died in a public place it was the law that he had to go to the city of Alicante for an autopsy, and that he could not be moved until the correct people came to transport him there. Meanwhile they had covered David with a sheet, but not completely. His feet were sticking out at the end. As I looked over at his body, I was horrified to see children playing in the sand right next to him. It was surreal. My other lady angel, meanwhile, had got three chairs from the chiringuito beach bar where they had been when they heard the commotion. She placed the chairs in a circle and advised me to sit facing away from the sea and more importantly, away from being able to see David's body.

One of the two ladies brought drinks, though I cannot remember what. They then started telling me all about their families and their problems, anything to distract me. Eventually an ambulance arrived and took David away. One thing I was thankful for that day was I had the card from the funeral plan we had purchased about a year earlier.

After that, one of "my angels" offered to drive me home in my car, with the other lady following to drive her back. In fact, that wasn't necessary, as just as we were getting ready to go, David's brother arrived. The policeman had encountered trouble finding their house, and then had trouble trying to make them understand what had happened. Bless him, he succeeded, as they followed him to the beach just in time!

I never saw my angels again, but did discover later they were real people, and worked at the same school as one of my friends. I was able to write them a thank you card, even though that seemed totally inadequate!

Mike, David's brother, drove me home in my car, and his wife drove their car. After a much-needed cup of tea, Mike offered to phone David's family with the news. I was grateful for this as I am sure I could not have done it. Over the next few days, the family started arriving from around the world. The irony was, most of them had been here two weeks before, for our ruby wedding anniversary, celebrating 40 years of marriage. However, some who had not managed to come that time, came now, including my daughter who lives in New Zealand, and my sister-in-law from Portugal. His funeral was held in a small open-air chapel in our village, followed by a wake in our home, mainly organized by my children.

David had a great sense of humor. He was good with people and good at seeing the big picture, while I was better at the day to day. He had an interesting life. He was adopted at age 3, in 1940, at the beginning of World War II. He grew up in Sussex, England. At 18, he joined the British South African Police, and went to Rhodesia. He served with the Rhodesian Airforce and later became a 'private eye.' During our married life we ran many businesses together, thus spending more time together than most couples with separate jobs. We made a good team, albeit with the usual ups and downs.

I did not expect to become a widow that day at the beach, but I often wonder if David had some sort of premonition. Shortly afterwards I wrote him a poem:

David, you left so suddenly, I didn't understand
Now I know you had to go that day upon the sand
I don't know why but can accept
Some things just have to be
The angels called you, and I wept
But now I clearly see
Your time was up, you had no choice,
You left with work well done
Your family collected here in joyful unison
And we, those loved ones left behind
To continue on the path
Of life, my friend, I now know why

We have to carry on,
Because all God's jobs, He gave to us
Have not as yet been done.
So help us angels on our way to carry on His task
In whatever way we can, until in glory we can bask.

Life Lesson: What I have learned from this experience is this. Don't let death take you by surprise. Repent daily, pray daily, get to know your maker, Jesus Christ. Live every day as if it is your last, because it may be, and one day it will be.

How to Find Meaning in Life
By Nancy Blodgett Klein

'Education is not just about going to school and getting a degree. It's about widening your knowledge and absorbing the truth about life."

—Shakuntala Devi, an Indian woman who wrote novels and texts about math, puzzles and astrology. She was popularly known as "the human computer" because of her ability to do complex math calculations in her head.

When I was a child, I didn't connect with school at all. I was one of those students who wasn't among the lowest performers in my classes or among the most gifted either. I was one of those lost-in-the-middle students. I can't remember the name of any of my elementary or junior high school teachers except one fifth grade teacher who was mean to me and other students. Her name was Mrs. Hagensen. We called her "Mrs. Hag-and-Bag." She told us "seems" was a ridiculous word. Something either *was* or *was not* the case. Even then, I knew enough about the ambiguity of the world to realize she was wrong about that.

After school, rather than doing homework or reading books, I would steal quarters off of my father's dresser and ride my Stingray bike to the local pharmacy to buy *Richie Rich* and *Archie* and *Veronica* comic books along with a bar or two of chocolate. I especially liked Nestle Crunch and Kit-Kat bars. My father worked full-time as did my mother so I wasn't closely monitored in terms of what I did after school. Eating all that candy caught up with me though: at one dental visit, the dentist informed me that I had 13 cavities!

I was the "baby" of the family and wasn't inspired to be a high achiever. I let my two older sisters pursue those roles. By the time I turned 12, though, I started to read some articles in the *Chicago Tribune* and that did interest me. There was also a class in social studies in middle school that intrigued me. We were learning about people and what they had done in the world. Now we were talking.

By the time I got to high school, I realized what captivated me most was people and what they thought and what they did in the world. It was in these kinds of classes that I found meaning. In particular, when I signed up for a Great Books course in high school, I got to read *Walden; Life in the Woods* by Henry David Thoreau. When I read the following quote, it was the first time I felt truly awake in school.

"I went to the woods because I wished to live deliberately, to front only the essential facts of life, and see if I could not learn what it had to teach, and not, when I came to die, discover that I had not lived. I did not wish to live what was not life, living is so dear; nor did I wish to practice resignation, unless it was quite necessary. I wanted to live deep and suck out all the marrow of life, to live so sturdily and Spartan-like as to put to rout all that was not life, to cut a broad swath and shave close, to drive life into a corner, and reduce it to its lowest terms..."

Now that sentiment was meaningful. "I wanted to live deep and suck out all the marrow of life..." Wow! Finally, this was something I could sink my teeth into. History was interesting, yes. But it also involved a lot of facts and dates. Reading what deep thinkers through history had to say about life was the moment when getting an education really mattered to me. I wanted to read lots more books by deep thinkers about life. So, naturally, when I went to college, I decided to study philosophy.

I read Plato, Aristotle, Saint Thomas Aquinas, Saint Augustine, Descartes, Hobbes, Hume, Hegel, Nietzsche, Kant, Sartre, Marcuse and so on. I studied other religions like Buddhism, Hinduism and Islam. My mind opened wide and took it all in. No more comic books for me. I was finally getting a meaningful education in a subject that mattered and still matters to me.

Life Lesson: This is a message especially meant for people struggling in school. If the subjects you are learning don't interest you, perhaps it is because you haven't yet been exposed to the ideas that matter to you. Keep educating yourself until you find that

subject that sets your mind on fire. It's out there somewhere. Have faith and keep reading! Also remember to brush your teeth!

A Prayer for Healing
By Nancy Blodgett Klein

Dear God, the prime mover of our universe

Help me to accept the passing of my loved one.

Grant me serenity to face each day with courage and acceptance of life as it is—a transitory place where those we love deeply may be taken from us at any time for any reason or no reason.

Help me to live life to the fullest, moving forward with love and gratitude, in spite of the challenges that we must confront each day.

The Golden Rule Doesn't Always Apply
By Darlene Foster

"The golden rule of conduct is mutual toleration, seeing that we will never all think alike and we shall see Truth in fragment and from different angles of vision."—Mahatma Gandhi

Like many of us, I was raised to follow the golden rule, to do unto others as you would have done to you. This is a good rule to follow, for the most part. We should never do something to someone we wouldn't want done to us. It is important to think about this rule whenever we need to make an important decision concerning another person. It is part of empathy, putting ourselves in another person's place.

But what if what you would like done to you is not what another person wants done to them? We are all different, from various cultures, family backgrounds, and personalities. We all have different wants and needs. This tapestry of differences is what makes the world an interesting place. So how can the same things possibly please each of us? For instance, my husband prefers a quiet birthday with just the two of us and not much fuss. I prefer a big party with many friends and family around. I often end up with a boring, quiet birthday and I sometimes make my husband a big party with many friends. I am doing for him what I want done for me! But that doesn't necessarily mean it's what he wants.

One time while vacationing with family, my aunt came down with a migraine while we were sightseeing. When we returned to the resort, she decided to go to her room and have a nap. When I have a headache, I need to lay down in a dark, quiet room and I don't want to be disturbed. The rest of us ordered pizza and congregated at one of the other units. A while later, my aunt arrived and was quite upset that we hadn't woken her up so she could join in. I wouldn't have done that as I wouldn't have wanted to be woken up if I had a migraine. I was simply following the golden rule.

I worked with immigrants in many of my jobs and quickly learned that cultural differences proved the golden rule doesn't always apply. Many things that a North American considers polite and appropriate can be construed as rude and inappropriate in another culture. For example, I was taught it was polite to shake hands upon meeting someone. When I extended my hand to a gentleman from another culture, he refused to shake my hand and said he could never touch the hand of a woman who was not his wife. I was taken aback, almost insulted. Later I learned this was part of his culture and I respected that.

A better rule would be, do unto others as they want done to them. The only way we can know what another person wants is to ask. This is where open communication comes in. One of the biggest problems is assuming one knows what the other person wants. How many marriages and friendships could be saved if people simply asked what the other person prefers instead of assuming what makes you happy will make the other person happy.

Life lesson: Although following the golden rule is advisable, it would be better to find out what the other person wants or needs before assuming how you wish to be treated is the same as how they wish to be treated. As Marian Beaman, author of *Mennonite Daughter: The Story of a Plain Girl*, noted, *"When you care about other people's welfare and background, you begin to accept their differences – even appreciate them."*

Life Should Be an Adventure
By Nancy Blodgett Klein

Life is either a daring adventure or nothing at all. —Helen Keller

My hubby and I both like warm, sunny weather so we decided to retire to Spain. Even though this is commonly done among British and Irish people, it's not so common among Americans. The Spanish government makes it hard to retire in Spain, throwing out lots of hoops for people to jump through. You have to prove you have never been arrested anywhere in the US. You have to prove you have no contagious illnesses. You have to buy a full medical insurance policy for a year, even before you have actually moved there. If you want to get a retirement visa or what they call a non-lucrative residency visa, you have to prove a certain minimum level of monthly income. When we applied for the visa, the minimum income level was a little below 2,200 Euros a month.

If you can't do all these things, plus spend money for a variety of fees and taxes, you can forget the whole thing. And everything they request must be translated into Spanish by a certified translator. Plus you have to have copies of everything and many photos of yourself. In short, you have to really want to move to Spain because retiring to sunny weather climates like Florida or Arizona are much easier. Just pack up the car and drive there. What is the big deal?

But we didn't want to move from one state to another to eat at the same chain restaurants we just left behind, such as Red Lobster, Olive Garden, Panera, and so on. We thought it would be fun to try paella, rather than pizza. We wanted to dive into a variety of tapas like jamon iberico, calamari or spanish omelets rather than order a burger and fries. We wanted an adventure, but nothing too extreme like backpacking across Afghanistan. We wanted to live in a safe, democratic country with warm weather, good music, lots of culture and history. So Spain fit the bill in all these ways.

Now that we are here in sunny Spain, we are glad we successfully jumped through all the hoops. It was well worth it. Every day is a new adventure, whether it be trying to get a Spanish drivers' license or having surgery in the hospital. Things are done differently here and that's what makes it great. You are not sleep walking through the day but navigating a roundabout with your eyes wide open looking out for drivers on the inside lane who decide to cut in front of you at the last second to turn right off the road. This makes for exciting driving. But it is not for the faint of heart. I have a North American friend here who doesn't drive beyond her neighborhood because the roundabouts are too scary for her.

Of course, lots of things are done differently here in Spain. For example, they traditionally eat much later. But the good thing about that is some restaurants offer early bird specials. So you can go to dinner between 5 and 8:00 pm and get the discounted three-course meal complete with a bottle of wine for 10 euros a person. In the US, if you want to partake in the early bird dinner special, you typically have to be in the restaurant and ordering by 6:00 pm, at the latest.

People are more relaxed about time here too. So if a Spanish electrician says he will be at your house at 10 am, don't be surprised if he shows up at 11:30 without explanation. This relaxed attitude rubbed off on us after living here a while, permitting us to enjoy the moment rather than continually checking our smartphones for the time.

Another bonus about Spain is they speak Spanish here. So if you move to Spain you have to learn a new language and that's good for aging brains like ours. Learning new things helps reduce the risk of dementia. Putting sentences together in Spanish and being understood by a native speaker is fun. It's almost like being a child again and learning how to read. New connections get made every day. For example, just a trip to the grocery store can be an adventure because all the spices have different names in Spanish than in English. So you have to fire up your smartphone app that translates words from Spanish to English to come home with the cumin you want rather than the coriander you don't need.

When you speak Spanish to a native speaker here, you typically get a warm response because you have made the effort, even if your pronunciation or grammar isn't perfect. At least you are trying and showing respect for the people in your adopted country. In general, when I do speak English here, Spanish people think I am from Canada. That's close enough to the United States, as far as I am concerned, because I am still learning to tell the difference between the accent of a Scottish person and an Irish one. As long as we are living, we should always be learning!

Life Lesson: If you want adventure in your life, be open to new challenges. Be prepared to leave your comfort zone in a variety of ways every day. Traveling to other countries or even living abroad is a great way to leave your comfort zone and experience life differently. So is trying new foods and learning a new language. Life is short. Make the most of it.

Step With Care and Tact into Life's Great Balancing Act

By Valerie Peachey, Ed.D.

"Oh, the Places You'll Go!

...You'll get mixed up, of course,

As you already know.

You'll get mixed up

With many strange birds as you go.

So be sure when you step.

Step with care and great tact

And remember that Life's

A Great Balancing Act.

Just never forget to be dexterous and deft.

And never mix up your right foot with your left."

—Dr. Seuss

Looking at life through a unique and somewhat eccentric lens, the words of wisdom shared here by Dr. Seuss, a famous children's author and poet, ring true. There are so many life lessons woven into this particularly imaginative book, *Oh, the Places You'll Go!*

The places I've gone have all been part of "Life's Great Balancing Act." Perhaps that is because I have been privileged to have lived and traveled around the world for the past 60 plus years. As a child, I was pale, blue-eyed, freckle-faced and blessed, some would say, with a mop of strawberry blond hair. An unusual sight when visiting villages in Africa, or as the honored guest to a certain tribe of Bedouins in the desert of the Middle East. Even as a far older adult I was somewhat of a curiosity with my now white-blond hair while traveling in India.

My father's career as a geophysicist required that our family be open to new adventures every few years. Constantly making new friends in various cultures, going to new schools every two years, learning to speak and write in different languages, giving up the past, not being rooted to a particular home, and discovering unique traditions did require care and tact and were indeed all part of "Life's Balancing Act." I grew to realize that constant changes were inevitable. I understood people in one part of the world did not always do things the way I had in the past. These continual changes and inconsistencies built my resilience to my many life adventures and optimistic outlook.

My varied experiences have led me to adopt an attitude towards life built on respect for differences, curiosity, and acceptance of the myriad of ways we choose to live in one world. We are all human beings travelling through our life journey as best as we can, while hopefully providing a smile, understanding and appreciation for each other.

Reflecting back on myself as a young six-year-old, my family and I were visiting a leper colony in the depths of Nigeria, on our way to one of my father's oil exploration camps. I had no idea what leprosy was and how it disfigured people. Left in the car, as my parents went to visit with the senior members of the colony, I remember being surrounded by dark disfigured faces and bodies. Skelton-like hands, reaching out to touch me, gaping smiles, eyes full of wonder, bodies full of crusty oozing sores, and flies enjoying a fleshy feast. Not wanting to appear rude, but being extremely scared, I smiled and tried to talk, hoping my mom and dad would quickly return. When they finally came back, we drove off to waves, smiles and much hooting and hollering. From this experience, I learned that gentleness and care are always understood. Of course, we are all different people living in different places, but kindness transcends language and race.

Several years later, camping with a tribe of Bedouins, in the dunes of the Libyan desert, we had settled in for the night under a crystal-clear desert sky. It resembled yards of black velvet encrusted with flawless diamonds. Heavy and well used Berber carpets, in tones of ruby reds and milky caramels, warmed the cooling sand inside the massive tent. The braziers were lit, the music started and the firepit was being dug up. It was time to eat. Massive platters of freshly slaughtered and roasted lamb, created specifically for this occasion of foreign guests, started to appear.

We all gathered in a circle, about 12 of us. Each person taking a handful of lamb and the traditional couscous accompaniment, with our right hands. Our Bedouin hosts welcomed us with toasts and warm words to the beat of traditional Arabic music. All of a sudden, with an immediate flourish, someone placed something in front of me that looked remarkably like an eyeball, albeit somewhat shriveled from cooking. Trying not to look aghast and hoping I wouldn't throw up, I smiled while simultaneously wondering "What's this for?" Then through gestures, more toothy grins and loud wailing music that rapidly increased its tempo, I got the idea that as the youngest guest, I was expected to eat it! What on earth!! How could I?

Not daring to insult our hosts, I reluctantly reached for the seeming delicacy, close my eyes and swallowed. Immediately this was followed by a well-deserved drink. Rounds of applause, more smiles and hugs from the women followed. Then, the meal continued, and I was able to eventually fall asleep as the belly dancing began.

From this experience and others, I learned that skin color, customs and culture can vary way beyond what we can imagine. But warmth, hospitality, respect and acceptance of differences build friendships and enable us to perform life's balancing act with care and tact.

As I ventured forth through my life traveling to a myriad of countries and places around the globe, I continued to learn how to effectively deal with "life's great balancing act." Wandering as a mature adult through a half-finished trade show area in India one afternoon, I caught sight of a young man sending me a wide smile as he worked on one of the display stalls before an upcoming large international conference. Not wanting to be rude and ignore him, I returned his smile. The following conversation ensued in lilting English.

"Madam, you have golden hair. It is so beautiful. I like it very much."

"Why thank you," I replied, a little unnerved but moved at the same time by his curiosity.

"Madam, may I touch it? I never see this before."

Pausing for a beat, I replied, "Really. Why yes, if you like, you can touch it." I bent down to let him stroke my head.

"Oh, Madam, thanks you, thanks you...I never forget."

"You are welcome," I replied. But I am the one who has never forgotten.

Life Lesson: Life can be a delicate balancing act. But if we keep open minds and open hearts, strangers can become friends while diverse cultures, traditions and customs can bring us cherished insights. Indeed, we can continue growing wherever we find ourselves in the world as long as we embrace differences with tactful diplomacy.

Be a Good Listener
By Nancy Blodgett Klein

"Listening is an art that requires attention over talent, spirit over ego, others over self." – Dean Jackson, author of The Poetry of Oneness: Illuminating Awareness of the True Self.

Have you ever noticed that most people aren't particularly good listeners? Typically, when I am at a party or other social gathering, the people I meet will talk about what interests them and not engage in a dialogue with you. A woman might ask what you do for a living and you say, "I am a teacher." "Oh, my brother is a teacher too," she replies. "He teaches math. But I was never any good at math." Where do you go from here? She asked what you do for a living but doesn't really want to know more about you. Rather, she is drawing a connection back to herself (her brother is a teacher) and she doesn't like math. Her ego is getting in the way of a meaningful dialogue.

Truly listening requires a deeper level of connection. In fact, don't talk to me about what you do for a living. Let's talk about ideas. What is important to you? What do you value? What gets your heart racing? Eleanor Roosevelt once said, "Great minds discuss ideas; average minds discuss events; small minds discuss people." Let's connect as two spirits in this great adventure known as life. Don't talk to me about all the expenses and hassle of maintaining your big house or name drop places you have traveled in the world. Tell me instead how you helped someone in need with your wealth or how you traveled across the world and escaped from danger because a kind local person helped you after becoming lost in an unfamiliar place.

Habit number four of Stephen Covey's book, *The Seven Habits of Highly Effective People,* is to, "Seek first to understand. Then to be understood." Many people seem to think it most important to tell their stories rather than understand the other person. What you say to another simply reminds that person of something else they want to share. "Oh, that reminds me of something that happened to me," someone will say. This is not genuine listening. Rather it can be a contest to see who can get the most words into a verbal exchange.

Being a good listener means paying attention to what the other person is saying, responding with appropriate questions like, "Was that upsetting to you?" or "You must be very happy about your daughter's new job." Listening means not judging, such as saying things like, "Wow. That really wasn't a smart thing to do." Listening isn't telling the other person how you have it worse off than they do. "You think your health is bad. Let me tell you what's wrong with me." Or "You think you have a bad boss. Well, listen to this..."

Listening is affirming the worth of the other person by paying attention to what they say and how they feel. Think of a conversation as you holding the other person's heart in your hand. You need to be tender and caring with that heart because deep inside is a small child wanting to be acknowledged. "Tell me about your day," you ask. And when your spouse or child tells you, you look at him or her and really listen. "Oh, you must be proud of yourself," you tell your son when he shows you a science test he got an A on. Or "That sounds really frustrating," you tell your partner after he tells you how his boss wasn't interested in his new idea to solve a problem at work.

Good listeners can summarize the key thoughts or feelings of the other person in their own words. When you do that, the other person will feel heard and may say, "Exactly," in response to you. As in, you captured just what I was trying to say.

When I lived in Limerick, Ireland, I participated in a workshop with an organization called Narrative4. The Limerick location is the first Narrative4 office outside of the United States. The organization was co-founded by Irish author Colum McCann and Lisa Consiglio. According to its website, Narrative4.com, the mission of this worldwide organization is to build a community of empathic global citizens who improve the world through the exchange of personal narratives.

This organization teaches people to deeply listen to a story about someone else's life and then the listener shares what was said in their own words to the group. Your partner then recounts your story in this public forum as well. Doing this was an immensely powerful experience. I could also see how it can be used to bring deeper understanding not only to two individuals but to clashing political parties or to nations in conflict, such as Israel and Palestine.

Many people are good at talking. Some can entertain you or even make you laugh. Others, unfortunately, make you long to be alone, where you can have silence and think your own thoughts or simply be in the moment. But it's a rare person indeed who is good at listening and able to hold their own ego in check long enough to make a deep spiritual connection with another human being.

Life Lesson: Learn to be a good listener by paying attention to others. Ask people questions. Respond to what they say to you with kindness and concern. Restate key thoughts of what they told you in your own words. This way the other person truly feels acknowledged. This is how you make meaningful connections. This is how you make good friends. This is how you make the world a better place.

How To Turn Dreams into Reality
By Darlene Foster

All our dreams can come true, if we have the courage to pursue them."
~ Walt Disney

As long as I can remember, I dreamt about writing a book. I envisioned holding the published book in my hands, reading it to children and doing book signings. But I always felt I was too busy with a full-time job, raising kids, dealing with aging parents, volunteer work and life in general to write a book. I used the excuse of *I don't have the time.* I kept putting it off, but the dream was always there, nagging me, begging to be pursued.

I took writing courses and had many ideas but never started putting them down on paper, as the idea of writing a book seemed insurmountable. I finally realized that like any large, time-consuming project, to make it happen I needed to break it down into doable amounts.

I set realistic goals with deadlines and wrote them down.

My long-term goal was to have a book completed in three years.

My mid-term goal was to write a chapter a month.

My short-term goal was to write for two hours a day, five days a week.

These goals were doable and by breaking them down into baby steps, writing a novel didn't seem quite so overwhelming. By writing them down, I had made a contract with myself, set them in stone, so to speak.

I also needed to set SMART goals to help me complete my first book.

S - Specific

I had to be **specific** in what I wanted to accomplish. Just saying *I want to write a book* is much too general. It would never happen. I needed to narrow it down to what kind of book and for what audience. Stating, *I want to write a book for children* was a good start. The more specific I became, the better chance I had of making that dream come true. *I want to write a book for children about a young girl who loves to travel and has adventures,* was better. But, *I want to write a children's book about a young Canadian girl who travels to the United Arab Emirates and has the adventure of a lifetime when she buys a mysterious perfume flask,* was the one that worked the best for me.

M - Measurable

I needed to be able to **measure** my progress in order to keep me on track. So I set benchmarks. My goal was to write 2 hours a day for 5 days a week. Those two hours included doing research and editing. My plan was to write a chapter a month. After 6 months I realized that although some months I managed to write a complete chapter, other months I didn't. That was fine, I just realized it was taking longer than I initially thought and readjusted my plan, giving me more time to do research and learn the craft of writing.

A - Achievable

A goal must be something you can actually **achieve**. The book I planned to write had to be on a subject I was enthusiastic about. If I had planned on writing a scientific book, that would have set me up for failure as I have no interest or ability when it comes to science. I do, however, love travel, adventures and children.

R - Realistic

I knew that when setting goals I had to be **realistic**. If I had set a goal to have a book written in one year and had never written a book before, have a full-time job, a family and a social life, I would not have been realistic. I gave myself three years for my first book as I had a very full and busy life with all of the above and more. Also, the learning curve was steep. By being realistic, I gave myself the time I needed and at the end of three years, I had the first draft of a twenty-chapter book completed.

T - Timely

Like most people, I work more efficiently and effectively when given a realistic **time limit**. By giving the completion of my book a specific, doable deadline, it was more likely to get completed. I heard someone say, *A goal without a deadline, is just a dream.* By giving up television for two hours every evening, I made the time to work on my novel. This soon became a habit.

Life happens of course and sometimes you have to readjust the deadline. SMART goals should be flexible. If I couldn't work on the story on a weeknight, I simply wrote for two hours on the weekend.

Life lesson: Meeting a goal like writing a book is hard work. There is no denying that, but as well as working hard, it is important to work SMART. In three years I had my first draft written. I have since written and published eight more books and a number of short stories and articles using this method of goal setting. Without it I would have never started the first book and would still be dreaming about writing a book. I have used this method of goal setting for other things in my life too, like retiring to Spain from Canada. As Colin Powell once wrote, *"A dream doesn't become reality through magic; it takes sweat, determination and hard work."*

We Are All Connected
By Nancy Blodgett Klein

"All things are connected like the blood that unites us. We do not weave the web of life, we are merely a strand in it. Whatever we do to the web, we do to ourselves." – Chief Seattle

The other day, I got to be a hero to two baby birds. I was outside getting into my car and the community association gardener was busy cutting fronds from the palm tree next door to our property. As I was pulling away to go to choir rehearsal, I noticed the gardener had cut off one of the fronds and it landed squarely in our back yard patio.

When I came home from choir after dark, I picked up the palm frond to take it to the garden waste bin and noticed something small and grey. I looked more closely and saw that it was two baby birds. They were so small that their eyes weren't even open yet. "Oh-oh," I thought. "I can't take these birds to the waste bin." So I fired up the computer and looked up what you are supposed to do about birds falling out of the nest. It said to put them within earshot of where they fell and wait for the mother to come back. I left them where they fell, since this was within sight and earshot of the palm tree they had fallen from. The next morning I looked out on to the patio and saw a full-grown Eurasian collared dove sitting on our fence. It was looking down at the birds but not doing anything to feed or care for them. After a while, it flew away.

By this time, I had gotten back on the internet and found a bird rescue facility about 45 minutes away. I called them to see if I could drop off the baby birds and they said they would take them. The woman said a lot more than that, but she was speaking Spanish very rapidly so I was only catching every few words. I think she was trying to give me directions but I thought I had this covered with Google maps.

I found a black rubber container that was shaped like a big basket and put a towel in it. With the help of my husband, Rick, we took the birds out of the nest and put them in the container. I drove to Murcia, where the center was located. But once I got there, I realized this place was massive and finding the rescue center could be a problem.

So I walked up to the first person I saw and showed her the birds and asked her where the center was. She told me it was further up the road. I noticed that she had about a dozen or so young people with her all wearing the same uniform. I thought nothing more about this but then heard about six or seven people running up behind me. This made me nervous so I kept walking. They didn't say anything intelligible to me. It seemed like they might have been developmentally-disabled young adults. Finally, I stopped, bewildered as to what they wanted. But it then became obvious that they just wanted to see the baby birds for themselves. So I let everyone have a look, waited for them to walk away, and then continued up the hill to the center with the birds.

Once there, a kind young man took the birds from me and asked me some questions about how and where I found the babies. In Spanish, the birds are called tortora turcas. In English, they are known as Eurasian collared doves. The birds had opened their eyes by now and I told the man they looked hungry. He said, "The vets will take care of them and feed them. Once they are big enough, they will be set free." 'Oh, joy,' I thought. 'Thank you, little birds, for giving me the opportunity to save you.'

On the drive home, I wondered why, of all the palm fronds that had fallen, just one would land in our yard and it alone would have tiny grey birds on it, sitting quietly beside each other in a straw nest. Did someone up there know I was a friend of the birds and would welcome the chance to be their savior?

Life Lesson: If you have the chance to help any living thing, don't hesitate to do so. We (humans, animals, plants) are all connected to each other. We are all responsible for the living things we encounter on this beautiful web of life we call earth.

Let Your Intuition Guide You
By Nancy Blodgett Klein

"Everyone who wills can hear the inner voice. It is within everyone."
—Mahatma Gandhi

GI Joe Figures, army tent and jeep

Sometimes our intuition or inner voice guides us to do the right thing after doing many wrong things. This is what happened to me back when I was a ten-year-old tomboy. My closest sibling was a boy and I liked doing boy things, as my older brother did. I liked wearing cowboy boots, climbing trees, playing softball and playing with Matchbox cars and G.I. Joes.

G.I. Joes are dolls designed for young boys, just like Barbie Dolls are designed for young girls. Rather than playing with a perfectly proportioned 12-inch plastic young woman and dressing her up in different clothes, I played with 12-inch plastic toy soldiers. I would dress them up in different army uniforms and have them use army paraphernalia like walkie-talkies and guns to fight imaginary battles with other G.I. Joes.

But my problem was I always wanted to get more G.I. Joe stuff than I had. So, to accomplish this without money, I would ride my bike to the nearby grocery store in Chicagoland (in this case, Jewel, a food store) and grab a brown-paper grocery bag. Then I would walk over to the adjacent store (Osco, a pharmacy with household items and toys) and help myself to G.I. Joe dolls, G.I. Joe tents, and related equipment. I would put everything I wanted in the brown bag, close it up and walk out the door, without being stopped.

This is shoplifting, of course. I knew it was wrong but couldn't seem to stop it. One day, though, I felt compelled by an inner voice to go to Jewel and Osco and steal more G.I. Joe equipment. This time, after I grabbed the paper bag from Jewel, I decided to steal a G.I. Joe Jeep. This was a big item wrapped in a big cardboard box that would undoubtedly be noticeable in the bag. But I wasn't too concerned about that. Instead, I was more concerned about the batteries the Jeep required. I decided it would be important to steal those first, slipping a package of AA batteries into my pants pocket before going after the bigger item.

Going back to the toy aisle where the G.I. Joe jeep was now that I had the required batteries, I picked up the box and shoved it quickly into the paper bag. I then walked out the door with the merchandise, as I had several times before. This time, though, a man followed me and stopped me. He confronted me with the stolen toy and made me come back into the store.

Since I was so young, the police were not called. Instead, my mother came to get me. I don't remember what she said to me about it if anything. We were a family that wasn't good at confronting problems head-on. Best not to discuss the big issues like my crime spree and pretend instead it never happened. I don't think she even told my father since he never mentioned it to me. I guess it was our little secret.

Of course, I was mortified by being caught red-handed. And that was the end of my shoplifting adventures. I think I simply had to get caught to stop doing something I knew was wrong. That's the day I also learned that I should pay attention to that inner voice when it tells me I must do something. Luckily, my inner voice has a conscience and it has never steered me wrong. Since then, I have stayed on the right side of the law rather than winding up in prison.

Have you ever had a similar experience, where your inner voice told you to do something and you did it and it led you down a different, better, life path?

Life Lesson: Let your intuition/inner voice guide your decision-making. Someone once wrote that using one's intuition is "seeing with the soul." I think tapping into your intuition is connecting with your soul. And if you believe in God, as I do, this soul-connecting work is how we get in touch with this source of all. If you aren't sure how to do this, I found it helps to spend some time alone, in silence, to better see with one's soul.

Volunteering is Valuable

By Darlene Foster

"People who volunteer tend to experience fewer aches and pains. Giving help to others protects overall health twice as much as aspirin protects against heart disease. This has a stronger effect than exercising four times a week." - What We Get When We Give by Christine Carter

For years I didn't do much volunteering as I had a pretty full plate already. Commuting over an hour each way to a high-pressure job in downtown Vancouver, raising teenagers, taking courses, attending meetings and spending time with friends kept me pretty busy. I barely had time to chat with my long-suffering husband. I always said, "Anything worth doing was worth being paid for."

I loved my job as a recruiter. Matching the perfect candidate to the perfect job was extremely satisfying. But it is a highly competitive business and things don't always go according to plan. I was feeling the stress. At one point, after suffering a couple of panic attacks, I was required to take a stress leave. My job was taking its toll on my marriage, my family and my health.

One day, as I was taking the bus to see a client, I happened to glance at the ads along the top of the windows. One caught my eye. It was for an immigrant services organization looking for volunteers to help families new to Canada settle in. I love meeting people from other countries and have always respected those brave enough to change countries for a better life. I jotted down the phone number before I got to my stop.

I called the number a few days later and made an appointment for an interview. Thankfully, they thought I would be a suitable volunteer. They liked my enthusiasm and the fact that I had a Teaching English as a Second Language Certificate. My first assignment was to help a Russian family that had just recently landed in Canada.

Ludmilla, a teacher, Gregory, an information technology specialist and their two teenage sons were delightful. We got along immediately.

I helped them find a family doctor, some second-hand furniture and a recreation center for the boys. They appreciated every little thing I did for them. Mostly we chatted over a cup of tea about the differences of the two countries and the similarity of our families. We also discussed books. They were pleased to hear that I loved Russian writers and they gave me a copy of Russian fairy tales. As we chatted, their English improved and they gained confidence. I helped Gregory write his resume and practice interviewing. It wasn't long before he found a job. I invited them over to our place for tea at Christmas so my husband could meet them and he gave them information on buying a second hand car. They eventually got better jobs, bought their own house and moved on with their lives.

I was later assigned to work with a Taiwanese woman and her small son who struggled on her own while her husband stayed in Taiwan. And I also helped a wonderful family from the Ukraine, both successful veterinarians who had moved to Canada so their eight-year-old son would have a better life. They were happy to take on menial jobs at McDonalds and as a pizza delivery person until they became qualified to be veterinarians in Canada.

It was such a rewarding experience. I met some amazing people, and it was good for my soul to see them appreciate things those of us born in North America take for granted. I learned a lot, my stress from the day job melted away, and my health improved.

Life lesson: Instead of thinking you don't have time to volunteer, think about the benefits of helping others. You will more than likely get more back than what you give. It is time well spent.

Be Open to Signs from the Spirit World
By Nancy Blodgett Klein

"And now here is my secret, a very simple secret: it is only with the heart that one can see rightly, what is essential is invisible to the eye."
—Antoine de Saint-Exupery

Some people say that a spiritual world doesn't exist because they can see no evidence of that. I say they aren't paying attention because the signs are there. After my dear mother died, I prayed constantly for a sign that she was alright, that she was in heaven and not just a pile of ashes stuck in a wall at her beloved Episcopalian Church. For months nothing happened.

In the meantime, I had joined a support group for adults who had recently lost a parent. I know some people don't feel the need for this, but I certainly did. Just because I was an adult, it didn't make my pain on losing my mother any less traumatic. Also, there are few people you can feel comfortable talking to about such an upsetting event. I have found people who are going through the same emotions at the same time as you can be the most helpful. We shared our sense of loss, our pain, our feelings of abandonment, our anger: whatever we felt or said wasn't judged. No advice was given. The trained facilitator just supported us in our grief and helped us to come to terms with our loss through the processing of our many feelings in a safe space.

After the one-night-a-week sessions ended after two months, some members of the group continued to get together for drinks and emotional support. On one of these occasions, one of my support group friends asked me if I had gotten a sign yet about my mother. "No," I said. "Still nothing." She replied, "You are going to get a sign and you are going to get it soon." "You sound pretty certain," I said. "I hope you are right."

The next day, I was driving my car to work and had WXRT on the radio. This is a popular rock and roll station in Chicago. They were playing the Credence Clearwater Song, "Bad Moon Rising." This song was too loud, too high energy for so early in the morning, so I turned off the radio rather than change the station to something more soothing. I continued to drive down the road with both hands on the wheel. I looked into the rearview mirror and noticed that the car behind me was getting too close and this started to annoy me. Suddenly, I heard the car radio softly playing music. I was really surprised by this since I had turned off the radio. So, I turned up the volume so I could hear it better. And wouldn't you know, it was harp music playing.

To me, this music is symbolic of heaven. It continued to play for at least five more minutes. When I pulled into the parking lot at work, a radio announcer came on and shared the name of the piece he had just played. The radio had switched to WFMT, a classical station I often listened to in Chicagoland. Now you might say, "Oh, you turned on the radio yourself and switched the station without realizing it," or some other nonsense. But this isn't what happened. The radio went from off to on, from loud to soft, from WXRT (91.5) to WFMT (98.7) by itself. You might find all of this quite implausible. But I took this as the sign I had been waiting for, the one that my support group friend had promised me the night before. My mother was with God and the angels, in heaven.

This musical message wasn't the only sign I received from the spirit world either. Several months later, I was feeling sad about the death of my mother, whom I had loved very much. A song she had taught me in kindergarten was running through my head. It goes like this: "Everybody come every day. Everybody come every day. We'll skip and run and have a lot of fun. So, everybody come every day." I guess this must have been taught to the kindergarteners to encourage regular school attendance.

I can't tell you why I was thinking of this song, but it made me miss my mom and I cried many tears that night. The next day, when I got up, I noticed two pennies on my dresser that hadn't been there the night before. I didn't think much of it, but when I went downstairs, there were three more pennies in the shape of a smile next to the kitchen sink. This did surprise me. Then I looked at the bay window behind the kitchen sink and saw another penny on the glass shelf in the window. Finally, I walked over to the kitchen table with my morning cup of tea and noticed a seventh penny on top of the wooden partition separating the kitchen from the living room. Seven is my lucky number.

That night, after we had both returned home from work, I asked my husband if he knew anything about the pennies and he did not. He hadn't known I was particularly upset about my mother the previous night nor had I shared that I had been crying. I like to do my crying alone, in private.

I took the seven pennies as a sign from my mother in the spirit world trying to let me know she was still around, watching over me, and trying to cheer me up. Remember three of the pennies were put down in the shape of a smile in a place I couldn't miss them, right next to the kitchen sink. Do you know the song, *Pennies from Heaven*? Well, it appears to have some basis in reality!

I googled *Pennies from Heaven* and found a site by Amanda Linette Meder that answers the question about why deceased loved ones send pennies to us. She said, "As for pennies, the meaning of number 1 is significant. The number one is usually associated with Oneness, as in One God, One Spirit, or One Body and One Spirit, where the human body and the human spirit are the same being. The number one means unity. Thus, pennies are symbolic reminders that there is unity in the afterlife, and a unity with yourself and your loved one visiting you - a oneness."

I don't know if Ms. Meder is right, but it does make sense to me. Another site I read on the internet said signs from heaven often involve electricity and the writer mentioned that you should "pay attention to the activities of your radio." Of course, you are free to not believe me. But usually when I share stories like these with other people, either they think I am nuts or more likely they will feel it's safe to share their own spirit world experiences with me.

Life Lesson: The spiritual world does exist. If you are paying attention, at some point in your life you will see signs from that world that are speaking directly to you. Be open to the signs.

Please Patronize Thrift Shops
By Nancy Blodgett Klein

"Second hand is the better choice of the whole wide world."
—Anonymous

Do you like to shop at thrift shops, or charity shops, as they are called in Europe? I like to shop at these places because the money you spend there usually goes to a worthy cause. In Chicagoland, I use to shop at and donate to a thrift store that benefitted battered women. The parent organization was called Wings, Women in Need Growing Stronger. Before we sold our house in the US, I think I must have taken at least 30 trips to this store to give away numerous bags of household items and clothes before we moved to Europe.

Here in the Costa Blanca (White Coast) region of southeastern Spain, near Torrevieja, there are charity shops to help abandoned dogs, cats, horses and even donkeys. Some of the shops raise funds to help retired people get out and do activities with others rather than be bored or lonely at home. There are also shops to help terminally ill patients receive in-home nursing care. In the area where we live, there are three retail shops that raise funds for Paul Cunningham Nurses Charity. The mission of this organization is to "assess and deliver high quality care to terminal prognosis patients in their own homes, free of charge."

English citizen Jennifer Cunningham founded Paul Cunningham Nurses Charity in memory of her son Paul. He died of spinal cancer after a long hard battle at the age of 33. According to the Paul Cunningham Nurses Charity brochure, "Jennifer first helped to nurse Paul in a cancer ward...On the Costa Blanca, there are no hospices and therefore often the patient and family are left to cope through to death unsupported either in the hospital or more often at home. Paul Cunningham nurses try to be there at later stages, free of charge, for the terminally ill. Already, they have helped many patients to die with dignity, peace and without pain."

This seemed to me to be a great cause so my husband and I signed up to volunteer there one day a week. That's one of the good things about being retired. You get to do things you never had time to do before. Since I had never worked in retail clothing before, almost everything about working there was new for me. We priced items according to set guidelines: for example, men and women's shirts were to be priced at 3.50 euros and up. Along with other volunteers, we figure out sizes of donated items, price them with tags, and then put them where they belong on the racks. We dress and undress mannequins. We organize books into fiction and non-fiction, English versus other languages. We accept, clean and put away household items, like plates and glasses. We ring up items at the register, accept money and give change. At the end of our shift, we print out a receipt showing the day's earnings and then put that money and the receipt into a safe for daily collection by a Paul Cunningham staff member.

The charity shop is open from 10 to 2 Monday through Friday. Our shift is every Thursday. During the shift, we always have good-hearted people coming in to drop off one or more bags of donations, so we spend a lot of time sorting clothes, pricing them and putting them out on the shop floor.

Many of our customers are English or Irish because the Costa Blanca area of Spain is full of English and Irish people. They get tired of all the rain in their countries and I can't blame them for wanting to be where the sun shines most every day. However, we get quite a few customers from Spain itself, as well as Germany, Scandinavia, Belgium and France. Some of our regular Spanish customers work at their own thrift shops and buy items to resell.

Whenever customers come in from Spain or France, I get to practice my Spanish or French and this can be the high point of the day for me. I get a chance to use the languages I studied in the United States in a real conversation with a native speaker!

The other bonus of volunteering at a charity shop is you get a first look at things that you might want to buy yourself for rock-bottom prices. We have bought shirts, shorts, pants, CDs, books, silver Swan-shaped napkin rings and a black cat statue for our patio.

In summary, there are bargains galore at thrift shops and all the money goes to worthy causes. What's not to like about this?

Life Lesson: The next time you pass a thrift or charity shop, please go inside to get some bargains and help others in need. Also, consider donating old clothes or household items to these stores rather than throwing them out. Reduce the waste in the world by reusing items rather than by buying everything new.

Pursue Your Dreams Whatever They May Be
By Maureen Moss

"Never give up on what you really want to do. The person with big dreams is more powerful than the one with the facts." –Albert Einstein

Nothing, absolutely nothing, can prepare you for the sight of Machu Picchu at dawn. You may have read about it. You may have seen pictures of it. You may even have tried to imagine what it feels like when you first catch sight of it. But the reality was beyond my dreams. Coming here was something I had always wanted to do. But the trek to the top was going to be challenging for me, I knew.

The first day of the four-day, 42-kilometre Inca trail had been easy - a gentle climb, not unlike a ramble on the English Lake fells. We followed the rushing Urubamba river, lunching after our first short climb by a waterfall, among four-foot high cacti and trees bearing fat, pink pods. By 5 p.m. it was dark and we had pitched our first camp in a muddy field, where enormous wild turkeys stepped haughtily among us. Sipping hot chocolate and nibbling popcorn, we discussed the dreaded second day: the hard, steep slog up Dead Woman's Pass. We crawled in to sleep at 8pm, tired and inwardly trembling.

The climb had started easily enough. After an hour or so, my breathing became more laboured. A woman passed me on horseback, and I was appalled to see porters, carrying several heavy packs each, running along nimbly in sandals, while the rest of us struggled to walk. The track rose steeply, so I made my way very, very slowly, concentrating on rhythmic breathing, and placing one foot directly in front of the other, up and up through the rainforest.

After nearly five hours of effort, I had reached the col, at 4,500 metres, but although my body was crying out for a rest, the wind was bitterly cold. I could not linger. I immediately began the descent, of almost the same distance as the climb. This was worse, as the path was uneven, consisted of small boulders, and included steps of over 1 metre deep. After a brief rest at one of the many Inca sites, the trail rose again for 400 metres, which by now felt easier. I was fortunate to have had two weeks to acclimatise, including a walk to a literally breath-taking 5,300 metres in the High Andes, one week before. Others were finding this second day a real trial, arriving at the camp several hours after the main party.

"Laydees and gentlemens, peek up ze laggages!" cried Mauro, our small but neatly-put-together guide, lifting his peaked cap to wipe his golden brow. The snow-capped peaks gleamed in the sunlight, while clouds rolled in at ground level between our tents. I watched the porters, cocooned in multi-coloured ponchos, crawling into caves to spend the night.

At first light on the third day, I managed to get speared by a piece of frozen grass as I attempted to pee between five layers of clothing. After a hurried breakfast, we plodded for fifteen minutes up near vertical steps to terraced ruins. This original path led us on over log bridges, through natural tunnels in the rock, and through the cloud forest, clinging possessively to the mountains.

Ancient steps were covered in lichen and lined with yellow orchids. The air was sweet with the scent of wild lupins. Bottle brush shrubs, fuchsia and hyacinths flourished. The only sounds were gentle birdcalls. The weather was perfect for walking, the sunlight caressing the landscape with maternal pride, while the trail itself was cool in the shade. The Urubamba snaked far below, as bright blue humming birds hovered in the emerald green of the vegetation. There are times when beauty is so overwhelming that the brain cannot find words to describe it adequately. Here, it was easy to believe you were in heaven.

We had to negotiate 5,200 steps down before we could rest our limbs at Winaywayna (Forever Young) hostel for the last night. En route, Mauro had expertly explained the purpose of each site and had related the engrossing story of the last days of the Incas. Despite several theories, it seems that no one can be exactly sure why Machu Picchu was built, nor why the skeletons found there were almost exclusively female. What is known is that the main gates are in line with the peaks of the greatest mountains. These were worshipped, along with Pacha Mama (Mother Earth), water, and Inti, the Sun.

In the hostel, after washing in what felt like liquid ice, I stepped over the exhausted bodies of dozens of walkers, huddled on the floor amid empty beer cans and crisp packets. I was grateful for my precariously perched tent, pitched on a metre wide ledge, with a three-metre vertical drop to the terrace below.

At 4:30 am the next morning, I struggled out of my sleeping bag and crawled out cautiously into the blackness, under thousands of stars, the tip of my nose tingling with frost. The porter had banged a spoon against his tin mug to rouse us. It was bone cold at minus 5 Celsius.

Today was the final day of the trail. After half an hour my 'mag' light's pencil beam was proving completely inadequate for the narrow, uneven path. Although there may be hundreds of people on the trail at any one time, for the most part you walk it alone, prey to doubts about your physical strength and receptive to the soul-soaring moments of achievement. I had taken a supply of the popular coca leaves to chew, plus Inti Raymi granola, chocolate bars and plenty of water. On this last morning I needed them all.

The highlight of the Trail is seeing the 'Lost City' at sunrise from the Sun Gate, about one hour's walk from the hostel at Winaywayna. I was keen to set off early in case my pace was not fast enough to reach the gate by first light. Now, as I stumbled along in the darkness, I began to fear that I had somehow trailed behind, as there was no sign of another torchlight. So, I quickened my pace, hoping to make out the shadow of someone up ahead.

The path was wet with dew. I shuddered at the sight of a sheer drop of some 15 metres to my right. There is a story that a lone walker had slipped from here, to be found eight days later with a snake nesting in his skull. By now I was seriously panicking, and I began to jog. In the half-light the torch was no longer needed, but it was this very light which worried me. How far was I from the gate? If it was already light, surely I wouldn't be there for the sunrise?

Then I ran, perspiration pouring, taking huge gulps of air. I had managed to get this far, still weak with amoebic dysentery, and I was not about to miss out on the climax. At times there was no path at all, or the trail disappeared into a log bridge, strung precariously from the mountainside. Breathless, but determined, I rounded what I was convinced must be the last bend, to face a 10-metre stone 'ladder.' I crumbled inwardly. I barely had the strength to lift my head, let alone force energy into my knees. But there, at the top, was a man squatting for a rest after the exertion of the climb.

"If he can do it, so can I," I thought. And I started up, breathing slowly. From the top, I could make out the shape, far ahead, of a pillar of stone, and shadows flitting about. One last effort and I'd be there.

The group was smaller than I expected, a dozen or so, staring silently out over the panorama. After panting for several seconds, I asked someone how soon the sun would illuminate the ruins, as yet still invisible below, in the shadow of the mountain.

"Oh, about half an hour. Plenty of time to rest," he said. I fell backwards in relief, laughing at myself secretly. I had run the last hour of the Inca Trail, to no purpose. I could have strolled and been there on time.

Suddenly, the light changed. Beams began to stretch down from the sky, marbling the mountainsides. A blink, and there it was, the famous silhouette taking shape before our eyes. Everyone drew breath and stood transfixed. In the silence, peace descended, enveloping us and uniting us in rapture, wonderment and veneration.

It is true. You feel the energy, you sense the magic. You leave, as Mauro said, 'con las piernas muertas, pero con el espíritu vivo' (with dead legs but with living spirit). My dream to see Machu Pichu had been realized and I would never be the same again.

Life lesson: Pursue your dreams and don't let anyone talk you out of them. Most importantly, don't talk yourself out of them!

Connect with Animals to Find Joy
By Nancy Blodgett Klein

"Petting, scratching, and cuddling a dog could be as soothing to the mind and heart as deep meditation and almost as good for the soul as prayer."

—Dean Koontz, American author

I was lucky to be brought up in a home with a dog. Our first dog was Dixie. She was a pure-bred collie we got in Virginia, a southern US state. Hence, the name Dixie. She used to chase me around the house, or I chased her. Can't remember which anymore. I do remember I liked to put on my blue overall snow pants when we would do our chasing game. Not sure why this was so important to me but I still remember hearing the *swish, swish, swish* of the pant legs brushing up against each other as I ran through the den, sun room, living room and front hall to chase her or be chased in an endless circle.

We also had dogs in the neighborhood. One nearby neighbor had a German Shepherd named Goliath. This dog followed me everywhere I went. His owner was a kind divorced woman who let him roam the neighborhood during the day while she was out at work. She didn't lock her front door either so Goliath could jump on it and push it open when he wanted to go back into the house.

Many times, he would get let into our house by one of my parents or one of the four of us children. Then he would go upstairs to my parent's bedroom and jump out one of the windows onto the roof. This slightly slanted roof over our sunroom faced the street. When Goliath would jump out there on hot summer days to survey the neighborhood, we would have people driving by stop their cars in a panic to run up to the house and yell, "Your dog is on the roof!" We would just say, "It's not our dog." And they didn't know what to say to that, so they would just walk away shaking their heads.

Goliath would also follow me to what we called the "five and ten" general store on Central Street in Evanston, Illinois. It was almost a mile away from our house. But Goliath would follow me there, crossing six or seven streets and walking just behind me. He was like my personal guardian. When I would go into the five and ten store to look for inexpensive things to buy, like cheap toys or candy, he would follow me in there too. The owner would say, "You can't bring your dog in here." And I would reply: "He's not my dog." Goliath wasn't my dog but he sure was my devoted friend.

Later, when I was married to Rick and our boys were six and nine, we got our first family dog. She was a yellow Labrador retriever who we named Molly. She was such a loveable dog who let the boys dress her up in Chicago Bears and Chicago Bulls sports jerseys. Our boys, Alex and Andy, liked to sleep on Molly's body while watching TV and she never objected. She never growled and rarely barked. Rick said that if a burglar ever came to the house, she would just wag her tail and show him around. Once we had to take Molly to the vet for what he called "happy tail syndrome." That's when a dog wags her tail so much that the tip of it bleeds from hitting things.

We all loved Molly very much and she loved us. She would always greet us at the door when we came home, wagging her tail vigorously. One of her favorite things to do was lick my husband's face. He liked that too. Ten years of joy later, when she got sick and I took her to the vet, we were all shocked and incredibly sad when he told us she had bleeding tumors around her heart, and it was making it hard for her to breathe. She had congestive heart failure and he said the best thing we could do was let her go because she would be suffering otherwise. This was very upsetting, and we all cried. As anyone who has ever loved an animal knows, the pain of losing him or her is very real and should never be minimized or dismissed with statements like, "It's just an animal" Or "Get over it."

We had a funeral service for Molly and buried her ashes and collar in our backyard in a ceramic bowl one of my sons had made. I read the Rainbow Bridge poem as part of the service. Its author is unknown.

THE RAINBOW BRIDGE POEM

Just this side of heaven is a place called Rainbow Bridge.

When an animal dies that has been especially close to someone here, that pet goes to Rainbow Bridge. There are meadows and hills for all our special friends so they can run and play together. There is plenty of food, water and sunshine, and our friends are warm and comfortable.

All the animals who had been ill and old are restored to health and vigor. Those who were hurt or maimed are made whole and strong again, just as we remember them in our dreams of days and times gone by. The animals are happy and content, except for one small thing; they each miss someone very special to them, who had to be left behind.

They all run and play together, but the day comes when one suddenly stops and looks into the distance. His bright eyes are intent. His eager body quivers. Suddenly he begins to run from the group, flying over the green grass, his legs carrying him faster and faster.

You have been spotted, and when you and your special friend finally meet, you cling together in joyous reunion, never to be parted again. The happy kisses rain upon your face; your hands again caress the beloved head, and you look once more into the trusting eyes of your pet, so long gone from your life but never absent from your heart.

Then you cross the Rainbow Bridge together.

Even though we vowed to never get another dog after losing Molly, we couldn't live without one for too long. So, a few months later, we drove to Save-a-Pet no-kill shelter and came home with an Alaskan Malamute named Sasha. She was a beautiful purebred dog that had been given up for adoption by a woman with three small children. She just felt having to deal with the dog plus all the small children was too much to handle.

Sasha was also a super mellow dog who never barked or growled. Like Molly, she would have invited in any burglar and showed him around the house. After being specially trained, Sasha became a therapy dog and I took her to a nursing home in Glenview once a month to visit the patients there. This brought the patients a lot of joy, to be able to pet Sasha and talk about the animals they had loved during their lives. Many of these patients were terminally ill so bringing a kind, furry dog to come visit them was a little something I could do to brighten up their days. I remembered with fondness how the hospice allowed both my parents to have their dog come visit them towards the end of their lives.

After Rick and I had both turned sixty, we were ready for a change of venue as our sons had both graduated from college and were now working. So, we decided to move abroad, first to Ireland and ultimately to sunny Spain. As part of the moving process, we had to give up Sasha and that was hard on us. We had rented a house in Ireland and dogs weren't allowed. Luckily, her new owner took good care of her and loved her as much as we did.

Once we moved to Spain, we decided our house wouldn't be a home without a dog. Rick also admitted that he wanted another dog to lick his face again! So, we went to a local rescue center called S.A.T. and asked if they had any friendly little dogs that were looking for a home. Out came Tess, a small mixed-breed black and brown terrier. First thing she did was jump up onto the seat where Rick was sitting and lick his face. So that was that! We took her home and never looked back. Unlike Molly and Sasha, Tess likes to bark and won't be showing any burglars around the house. In fact, whenever she passes a big dog on the street, she almost always barks, just to say, "I am not intimidated by you." We call this small-dog syndrome.

Given our ages, Tess is probably the last dog we will ever have. Of course, we said that when Molly died and when we had to let go of Sasha. So, I guess you never know. One thing I am sure about, though, is that dogs are a great source of comfort and joy. They love us unconditionally and that makes them very special indeed.

Life Lesson: Get a pet to love, preferably one from a shelter rather than a pet store or breeder. Dogs are nice and will probably

love you from the get-go. Cats typically take longer to warm up to people, but they can be lovely pets too.

Ask for Directions
By Nancy Blodgett Klein

Question: Why does it take millions of sperm to fertilize one egg?
Answer: Because they won't ask for directions!

Have you ever noticed how some people are scared to ask for directions? They don't want to look like they don't have everything under control so they just muddle through to get places rather than asking someone who might know. Sometimes people just want to appear confident to others, so they pretend to know what they are doing when they don't have a clue. Although not asking for directions is something men commonly do, I used to be like this sometimes too.

In fact, while I was in college, I was lucky enough to be able to spend a semester abroad in Aix-En-Provence, France. It's a beautiful city in southeastern France with tree-lined streets and many beautiful water fountains. My American roommate Martha and I lived on the outskirts of town and rode mopeds to get to school during the week. The family we stayed with told us we should go exploring on the weekends and see that part of France. We took their advice and rode our mopeds to nearby Mount Saint Victoire. This is a mountain that French Impressionist Paul Cezanne painted when he lived in Aix-en-Provence. Cezanne was born in Aix in 1938 and died there in 1906.

We decided to climb Mount St. Victoire one weekend. I remember that I was dragging along my crash helmet and was wearing a backpack that had a hardbound copy of *The Rise and Fall of the Third Reich* in it. I guess I thought I was going to do some serious reading during our little adventure. I remember we bought a baguette, some ham, cheese, a bottle of red wine and one of water and a bar of chocolate and stopped for a picnic part way up the mountain. It was a

happy memory and we didn't get lost.

Me at 20 years old on top of Mont St. Victoire outside of Aix-en-Provence, France

Another time the French family suggested we take a train to Briancon to go skiing. We finally took their advice and tried to go there during the winter of 1977. However, when we got to the train station in Aix, a train pulled up that was going to another town that was spelled similarly to Briancon. Rather than ask someone if it was going where we intended, I told Martha we should get on because we didn't have time to ask for directions. Never mind that the train was going south instead of north!

Of course, we didn't know this at the time. We just settled ourselves in for the long ride to the town. Weren't we surprised when the train stopped at a town and everyone got off? Then the lights went out. Finally, a janitor came in to clean the car and looked surprised to see us there.

He told us this was the end of the line and took us into the station. A middle-aged man there offered to give us a ride to another train station where we could get a train to Grenoble. This was a big city northwest of our intended destination of Briancon. But we were assured that there were plenty of places to ski there since Grenoble was by the French Alps.

When the good Samaritan was about to drive us to the other station, he suddenly got out of this car on a hill and forget to put his emergency brake on. The car started to roll backward with us in it. I realized then that we were in for some adventure! He ran towards his car and was able to catch up to it before we crashed backwards into another car in the parking lot.

Once we arrived at the large train station in the coastal city of Marseille, south of Aix, we had to wait there until midnight to take an overnight train to Grenoble. While there, we saw a drunk man trying to eat a china plate. This upset Martha, who was a more sensitive soul, while I saw some humor in the situation. We moved elsewhere.

While at the Marseille station, we managed to buy tickets for the proper train, one actually going to Grenoble. However, we didn't realize that with an overnight train like this we would need to reserve a specific place to sleep. Once on board, people in most every car said no, we can't sit with them. Luckily, a group of young girls on their way to compete in a basketball tournament took pity on us and let us share their cabin.

Once we got to Grenoble, we found a cheap place to stay at a ski resort called Alpe D'Huez, just east of the city and right in the French Alps. We planned to go skiing the next day. But that night we had pizza for dinner and there was olive oil on the table to go with the pizza. For some reason, I put oil on the pizza, as if it didn't have enough on it already. I didn't taste any difference, so I kept putting on more oil. I thought having extra oil on pizza must be some sort of French culinary tradition that I was not aware of. And I was trying to go native.

The oil-soaked pizza didn't agree with me, so I woke up sick as a dog. Martha went skiing without me. After we had come so far, I was bound and determined to go skiing too. So later in the day, I bought an afternoon lift ticket and went down the hill once or twice but was too sick to continue. How dumb! Plus buying the lift ticket used up my money.

The next morning, after we left our spartan accommodations, we had to find our way back to Aix. However we were out of money. So, we walked as far as we could and then decided to hitchhike. I don't recommend this but when you are young, you do stupid things. While we were hitchhiking, one van full of young men tried to run us off the road. We both dived into a ditch to avoid getting hit.

Even after this happened, we kept walking down the mountain and trying to hitchhike because we were out of options. Most of the time, we did get rides without incidents. However, on our last ride, the man offered to drive us all the way home. This sounded fine to me. It was late in the day and we wanted to get home since school started up again the next day. I climbed in the front passenger seat, since my French was better than Martha's, and she got in behind me. I talked to him as we drove through the French countryside and he seemed friendly enough. He even wore a French beret.

When we were a few kilometers away from our French family's house, however, Martha grabbed my left shoulder and pulled it back and forth really hard and yelled, "He's exposing himself!" Oh no. Now I had to prepare myself to look and see if this was really the case. It was. The man was hitting his upright member while saying, "C'est jolis, n'est pas?" No wonder he wanted to drive us all the way home!

What this pervert was saying in French means, "It's pretty, isn't it?" Oh my. I begged to differ. I told him we would be getting out right there, not a few kilometers later at our intended destination. Thankfully, he let us out without incident. After that, if either Martha or I wanted to make each other laugh, we would say, "C'est jolis, n'est pas?" Quite the memory. Although I could have done without the whole sorry experience, it did teach me the importance of asking for directions so I could get on the right train.

Life Lesson: While traveling in an unfamiliar place, ask for help if you aren't sure how to get where you are going. For example, don't assume when a train pulls up at the station, that you are on the correct side of the track before boarding. Ask someone. This will save you lots of aggravation.

Mourn losses, accept life's fragility, but embrace living anyway

by John Edwards

"Death is not the greatest loss in life. The greatest loss is what dies inside us while we live." —-Norman Cousins, American political journalist

It was my fifth summer of life. It could have ended that sunny June afternoon in a rough stony farmyard in Herefordshire, England but it didn't. A maybe inspiring primary school attendee was no match for the metal rear end of an American Case tractor. Life suddenly went on with me standing in the stone sink with my forehead being bathed in cool hill water by the dairy maid, Marjorie. My first ever trip in a car being driven by the farmer, Sid Cooke, who wanted his hay baled. Instead, he ferried me to the surgery where I sat in a chair and received two stitches. I don't recall any pain or discomfort or at least my memories refuse to tell me.

Am I hard-headed or what? I have asked myself. It was said that my male frontal lobes protected the delicate interior from any trauma and I lived on. Stubbornness may have lived on in me too! It wasn't life changing, as such, but it was a day that marked my existence. That simple fact that I can recall it so well is significant. It has been an important thread in my life and one that will re-occur. I knew from an early age how fragile life is and how it can end. Resilience is important.

I suppose that was my first recollection of care and a showing of love that I can now articulate. Looking that long way back I had cartloads of love and care which I realised but of course, that sat along everything else going on in the life of a soon to be five-year-old.

There were four of us in the cottage, two upstairs and two downstairs, until my paternal grandfather died upstairs in his bed. I was eight. I knew what was going on and I knew what I was doing when he died. It is not for inclusion here but I wrote a poem about it. I don't recall my feelings at the time and I presume a degree of self-protection takes away the angst. I remember my father's distress and the imbalance it caused in our fragile family economics. It was decided - parents know best of course - I would not attend the funeral. I wanted to. I knew what was going on and I wanted to be part of it. The poignancy of it is never to exclude. The option to be included helps to create the feeling of belonging, of being part of one family and of being loved. I have never forgotten their decision although I know they were making it for me. That's love, of course, and that exemplifies the overuse of the word, "No," in parental speak.

Moving decades on I remind myself of the first chapters in Professor Dame Sue Black's book, *All That Remains*. Her first three chapters should be in any school curriculum. She delicately but candidly deals with loss and how death is dressed up with other ways of describing it. Now, in later life, the value of being honest about the significance of death and the process of travelling through the emotions of grief cannot be overstressed. It probably won't ease the pain and it really shouldn't because that is part of the process as I have come to understand it. This is one 'life lesson' that matters so much and for some, it is one that is difficult to talk about. For others it's taboo.

In life, there is a propensity for caution. There are times when it is absolutely necessary to be cautious but if we listened all the time to the overly cautious would anyone do anything at all? It's a question I still struggle with today because my 34-year-old wife, who for health reasons wasn't allowed to participate in physical activity in her school days, had 'anchored' in her mind the desire to ride a horse. She did that and rode out one day. The horse came back and she didn't. That was the hardest and most painful day of my life. With one disastrous event, I had lost my wife, my lover and my soul mate. She had so much to live for. It has been a hard lesson to work through, accepting that her death was the result, but she died doing something she wanted to do. In a general sense, a long-held regret could be corrosive and so restrictive and even demoralising for one's life to be happy and contented. Yes, life is fragile and fragility should be respected but never to the extent of a life not being allowed to exist in contentment. Should someone have told her, "Don't ride that horse!" And what would have followed then? Sometimes, I believe in following one's nose or, if you prefer, one's instincts.

Life lesson: Life is a journey and not every pathway will be a correct one. That sums it up for me because not everything will be successful. Regret what you will, but regrets can be viewed in the positive for who we are today is because of all our yesterdays. Caring for others and loving life is as important as loving our beautiful world. We must have a healthy planet and more minds need to re-set to ensure that happens. It is essential to support the environmentalists and everyone who cares about conservation.

Retirement Requires Rebirth
By Nancy Blodgett Klein

Life is all about balance. You don't always need to be getting stuff done. Sometimes it's perfectly okay and absolutely necessary to shut down, kick back, and do nothing. –Lori Deschene, author of Tiny Buddha: Simple Wisdom for Life's Hard Questions.

Being retired is like being a child again, where you get to do whatever you want when you want. Only now you have money too! At least, that's true for the lucky among us who do have enough money to not worry about it. I have some friends in their late 60s who are still working because they have no other choice. I feel bad for them because they don't have the freedom to stop.

But actually being retired has its own challenges. I used to be a public school teacher and even though this job could be incredibly stressful and exhausting, it is meaningful. You really are making a difference in the lives of young people.

When you are retired, however, you must begin again. You must find things to do that give your life meaning. Undoubtedly having grandchildren would give life meaning. But you can't just wait around for your children to have children of their own. This might not happen soon, or it might never happen.

You must make your own choices. And if you are anything like me, having too much free time is a scary prospect. I thrive on having a lot to do and am not really comfortable just being. Retirement forces choices upon us. You must decide what to do with endless free time, where every day is effectively Saturday. My husband, Rick, is comfortable with retirement. "I have all the time in the world to do absolutely nothing," he jokes. But he has always been comfortable with being, rather than doing. He has taken to retirement like a duck to water. Me, not so much. I have always felt driven to accomplish things. Life is short. I have to make a difference while I am here. My relationship with time is not so relaxed.

Knowing that I have this drive to accomplish things that doesn't completely go away when one is retired, I have joined two choirs and two book groups. I love to sing with others, and I love to read and talk about books with avid readers. I have also chosen to do yoga for the good it does for my aging body and restless mind. It is also a great place to make friends. When I lived in Ireland, I found my best friends in yoga class. And I have made good friends in yoga now that I live in Spain.

There is something about people who practice yoga that speaks to me. Perhaps they are more open and spiritually aware than some others. The half-hour of meditation that we do in yoga helps me to be in the moment, rather than think about what I need to do next. It helps me shed the working mentality I used to have about task completion. In the past, a day wasn't worthwhile unless I had accomplished many tasks.

Retirement requires you to slow down and enjoy the day. It also helps you start jettisoning all the shoulds and should nots that swirl around in your mind. "I should clean the house." "I should not sleep in." "I should go grocery shopping." "I should not watch TV during the day."

Retirement can allow you to say goodbye to shoulds and should nots. You can give yourself permission to become a new person that is comfortable reading a novel rather than just non-fiction books. Now you can walk on the beach for no particular reason rather than run a required errand. Now you have time to stop and admire the beauty of flowers in bloom rather than feel the need to trim the bushes.

I am still not 100 percent comfortable with retirement and part of me keeps thinking the vacation will end and I will have to go back to work, go back to the person I used to be. But now I think my most important "work" is to be okay with sitting in silence, to be okay with not going anywhere, to be okay with doing absolutely nothing.

As the Buddhists understand, such a quiet place is where you find yourself. And if you are open to it, this place of silence is also where you can connect to the holy, to the world of spirit. And in the end, this is where I always wanted to be.

Life Lesson: Retirement is not for the faint of heart. It requires growth and change. One must be willing to be born again, with a new, post-work, identity. One is constantly challenged to find a balance between doing things that give one's life meaning and purpose and sitting still, doing nothing, and being okay with that too.

Attitude is Everything
By Nancy Blodgett Klein

"Your living is determined not so much by what life brings to you as by the attitude you bring to life; not so much by what happens to you as by the way your mind looks at what happens."

—Khalil Gibran, Lebanese author of The Prophet.

One month into the Covid-19 lockdown in Spain that began in mid-March 2020, I saw my English neighbor Ray walking his white terrier in a park near our house. I, too, was walking our dog, Tess, a mixed-breed black and brown terrier we got from a rescue shelter. Standing about one meter apart, as required by law, Ray asked me how I was doing.

"I am so bored," I replied.

"Really. I'm busy."

"What are you doing?" I asked.

He had built bookshelves next to a mailbox nearby so people in the Los Dolses community could donate books as well as find books to read. Before he replied, I thought, perhaps he is busy doing similar projects at home.

"Well, I'm reading books," he said.

"Me too," I replied.

"And I'm watching some movies," he added.

"I'm doing that too."

"I'm taking my dog for walks."

"Me too."

"Don't you miss going out to eat at restaurants or having a drink at a café?" I asked.

"Of course, I miss that. But I don't think about that now. I think about what I have, rather than what I am missing."

Well, I thought. Ray is teaching me a lesson here. I need to focus on what I have right now and be grateful for that, rather than suffer by focusing on what I am missing. He is keeping busy doing the exact same things as me and says he is busy rather than bored! I took that as a sign that I needed to focus more on what I am grateful for and not on what I lack during the strict government-imposed lockdown.

Here is what I am grateful for:

- I am still doing yoga but now it's on Zoom via teacher-led instruction rather than in person.
- I am in good health as is my husband. Two people we know have had Covid-19. (Later on during the pandemic, we learned of at least 20 friends or acquaintances who had contracted Covid-19). One of the first two people we knew who had the virus was hospitalized in Scotland. She said she had never felt so bad in all her life. The other person we knew, an English man with a bad cough, chills and a high temperature, was told not to go to the hospital in Torrevieja because there were too many people already there with the virus.
- I am not dealing with this lockdown alone. I am facing it with my husband of 32 years. I know three women in my choir who are dealing with this alone. All three of them are widows whose husbands died in the last three years.
- We are retired and have enough money coming in from our pensions and social security that we can weather this economic storm. Many people we know are struggling and money is very tight. Some have lost jobs and have little or no savings to tide them over. Plus, they may have children to feed. This is a much more difficult time for them. It's not about missing a planned vacation trip. It's about survival.

Life Lesson: During a pandemic or any stressful times in one's life, it's really important to be grateful for what we do have. The lockdown in Spain didn't last forever. But an attitude of gratitude is

always a good idea. Most especially, this is important during times of adversity.

Don't Make Fun of Other People
By John McGilvary

"Do as you would be done is the surest method I know of pleasing."
—Earl of Chesterfield

I recall when 'I Remember You' was top of the charts, or, more accurately, the Hit Parade, as it was known in 1962. The yodelling Australian had shot to the number one spot that summer. This year was also memorable as it was my first holiday without my parents.

I was attending a Boys Brigade 'camp' situated in Turnberry, Ayrshire, in Scotland. The term camp was a bit of a misnomer. Not for us a life under canvas like the Boy Scouts, rubbing sticks and intoning strange chants beside the resulting campfire (which I suspect owed more to Swan Vestas matches than to elbow grease). Oh no, we were all dressed in sparkling clean white belts and shiny brass buckles and had the relative comfort of dormitory living. We also had that unique sense of freedom, which only the removal of parental control can induce. Admittedly, the officers in charge of us imposed rules and regulations but, all in all, it was a fairly easy-going regime. Plenty of physical activity by day and endless games of cards (no gambling) in the evening.

One of the most popular card games that we played was called Switch, the rules of which are lost in the mists of memory. The officers sometimes joined us and there was often good-natured banter when they lost. One officer in particular lost more often than most. In fact, he didn't win a single game, so by the end of the first week, someone had coined the nickname 'Wee Switch' for him, which, to his everlasting credit, he accepted in good humour.

On the last night the boys, mainly fifteen- and sixteen-year-olds, had to put on a show for the officers. I, in my role as a budding Paul McCartney, wrote some alternative words to a song that was racing up the Hit Parade called 'Big Bad John' and named it "Wee Sad Switch." I sang it to the accompaniment of howls of laughter from boys and officers alike. Halfway through my rendition I glanced at "Switch" to see how he was reacting and saw a fixed grin on his face which didn't quite hide his acute embarrassment. But with all the insensitivity of a teenager, I plunged on regardless and revelled in the applause at the end.

Fast forward twenty odd years as I boarded the tube (known colloquially as the Clockwork Orange) in the centre of Glasgow. As I took my seat, I realised that the man sitting next to me was none other than "Switch." We started jawing about old times, punctuated by a few laughs, but never mentioning Turnberry 1962. Suddenly I realised I had reached my stop and the doors were beginning to close. I leapt from my seat and just made it onto the platform. I stood there as the tube moved off slowly and, glancing through the window, saw Switch still talking animatedly to his now absent companion.

Suddenly he saw me outside and I saw the same look of embarrassment flit across his face. Something bubbled up inside me, the wild urge to howl with laughter at the absurdity of the situation. Instead, a mirrored sense of acute embarrassment stole over me on seeing his discomfiture. I gave him a weak wave and walked swiftly along the platform. Perhaps the boy had grown up somewhat. At least I like to think so.

Life Lesson: Making fun of other people can be hurtful. Don't do it. Sometimes we have to grow up to realize these truths for ourselves.

Beware of Online Imposters Posing as Big Stars
By Nancy Blodgett Klein

Even loss and betrayal can bring us awakening." — Buddha

I have an Instagram account that I use to keep up on what our two sons and other family members are doing. It's really fun to see photos or short videos of family there and I look forward to their latest posts. However, there is a down side to Instagram and other social media that I recently learned about the hard way. I was on Instagram recently and noticed that famous Irish actor Liam Neeson was following me! That certainly got my attention because I have a big celebrity crush on him. This has been the case since Neeson appeared as Oscar Schindler in *Schindler's List* back in 1993. So I have had a crush on him for 28 years.

Anyway, when I saw that he was following little old me, I wrote to his Instagram account and asked if it was really him on the account as I had a big crush on him. He wrote back and said it was him and he was just reaching out to his fan base. Thus began a one week trip down the rabbit hole for me. We wrote back and forth to each other for a week, both asking many questions of each other, some personal, like how many siblings do you have, and some general, like what's your favorite food?

When I asked Liam (at least that's who I thought it was at the time) what his favorite movie was, he never said. Rather than take this as a warning signal that this wasn't him after all, I rationalized that he wouldn't want to tell me because this would upset the producers and publicists of any movie he didn't say was his favorite. He was writing to me so much that I started to think it was creepy. So I took a break for two days and then I decided maybe Liam was just lonely and looking for a friend, someone who would see him as a person, not as a celebrity.

So I wrote him and said the following: "Hi Liam. I was thinking about you and wondered if being so famous makes it hard to make good friends because people cannot see past your celebrity to the person within." He replied, "You are right. I'm happy that you could understand what I go through in life, being a celebrity isn't that easy. Sometimes people don't really understand how you feel. They forget you're a human being."

He added, "My wife was my best friend, she understands me and I shared almost everything with her. It still hurts my heart that she's no more. I still hope and wish I can find a true friend who will see me as a human being but not as a celebrity." (Neeson's wife died tragically in a skiing accident in 2009.) This reply tugged at my heart strings to hear that Liam was still sad about the death of his wife and lonely too. I let my heart take over then and lost my head.

This person sent me a photo of himself to prove that he was Neeson. He was holding a dog in the photo and it definitely looked like the famous actor. He also shared more about what he was looking for in a relationship. "My late wife and I were good friends before we got married, we sacrificed a lot in our friendship before we even thought of dating and getting married. Our friendship looked like we were already in a relationship. That's the type of friendship I want." Of course, I replied I was happy to be his friend.

As friends do, we kept communicating for a few more days. He found out I was a writer who had just published a book. He asked to see it and gave me his email address. I sent him an electronic copy of the book and he said he thought it was really good and added that he could help me promote it to a publicist he knew. Of course I was thrilled with that. After he claimed to have read my book, he said it deserved the best promotion and that his publicist would help make that happen.

Of course this was all too good to be true, but I didn't want to see that. He send me a poem too. Here it is:

Good morning, my Friend

I just want to say

I hope you have

A Beautiful day

And as the sun

Rises in the sky
The clouds I see
Are passing by
And on each cloud
A wish for you
That you'll enjoy
All that you do
And know you're loved
In every way
I hope you have
A beautiful day

He also sent me two photos he claimed were from the set where he was shooting. He said he was filming a movie in Australia and it was a love story. And on and on it went, with each of us sharing likes and dislikes with each other until he suggested we get together sometime. We are going to California in the fall and he said he was doing a film in California later this year. So before I suggested meeting him, I wrote my sons and asked them if they wanted to meet Liam Neeson. That's when our younger son Andy called me right away and said, "Stop communicating with whoever this person is immediately. It's not Liam Neeson!"

So I have Andy to thank for helping rescue me from the rabbit hole I fell down into. Thankfully, I never shared any financial information with this person. That really would have gotten me concerned. Maybe this celebrity imposter just thought this was all innocent fun or perhaps he or she was waiting to develop my trust enough to ask for personal financial information further into the relationship. There are many reasons why people do unethical things, like pretend to be someone they are not. I won't hazard a guess here. I can only reflect on my own role in this experience.

Until I decided to write a post about this upsetting experience, I didn't even realize that this imposter had misspelled Liam's last name on the Instagram account. He or she had written Liam Nesson, not Liam Neeson. I am sure the real Liam Neeson knows how to spell his name. Since I cut off communication with this unethical person, he later sent me a photograph of what he claimed was Liam Neeson's driver's license. It was actually funny because the license had clearly been altered. It had a Brooklyn, New York address for the actor who actually lives in upstate New York. His name is spelled wrong on the license, spelled Nesson, not Neeson. And to top it off, according to his license, Liam Neeson's sex is female. And we all know that's not true!

According to an article I read on this topic, people imitating famous celebrities online is a common problem. One of the things the article said is that celebrity followers are "sitting ducks" for the impersonators who want to exploit them and their desire to connect with a celebrity. I guess I was a sitting duck, at least for one week. This experience taught me to be really careful about who you connect with online. It hasn't changed my feelings for Liam Neeson, though. I don't think that crush is ever going away.

Life Lesson: If something seems too good to be true, it probably isn't! If you have doubts about someone or something, ask people you trust what they think before you share any personal information.

There is Something Special About the Irish
By Nancy Blodgett Klein

"There are only two kinds of people in the world. The Irish and those who wish they were." – An Irish saying

Before retiring to Spain with my hubby Rick, we lived in Ireland together for more than one year. While working as a database administrator for a big Chicago bank, Rick had heard about an opportunity to transfer to a position in Limerick and he asked me if he should apply for it. I said sure, as I was ready to leave Chicago and its terrible winter weather. So he moved "across the pond" in January 2016 and I joined him six months later after retiring from my teaching position and selling our Chicagoland home.

Thus began our adventure. We really knew extraordinarily little about the Emerald Isle before moving there. I had traveled there once before with my mother and could see that it was a very green place and knew that Dublin was its biggest city. I had also heard of William Butler Yeats, an Irish poet, as my mother wanted to visit a place that commemorated him when we visited in 1980. She was a high school English teacher and knew about such literary greats as Yeats. Back then, I also learned we had relatives from Ireland on my mother's side of the family, including in Dublin and in the town of Armagh in Northern Ireland. Since my mother died in 2004, going back to Ireland was also a good way to reconnect with my memories of us there together. So, without further ado, here's what I learned about Irish people through living there.

They are among the friendliest people in the world. The Republic of Ireland only has about 5 million people in it. Chicagoland, by contrast, has 9.5 million people. Ireland is a small country, where people treat each other with kindness and respect, almost like you are a member of one big extended family. At least, that was my experience.

Irish people are funny too and have no problem making fun of you or themselves. They never seem to be haughty or full of themselves.

One of my favorite books is *Angela's Ashes* by Frank McCourt. His memoir of his life in Limerick was full of humorous stories. Of course, it was also quite sad at times, given the death of several family members and the grinding poverty he experienced as a child.

Irish people love music too and enjoy getting together to perform it. There were so many pubs in Ireland where you could go for a pint and watch live music performed by a variety of talented musicians at no charge. This has to be one of the best things about visiting this beautiful country.

Irish people, in my humble opinion, are friendly, funny and love music. Of course, there are exceptions to any generalization about people from one place. But this was my impression of Irish people while living there. Here are some experiences I had that illustrate their friendliness. I took a weekly yoga class in Limerick and made several friends there. In time, I was invited to an art show opening for one of the yoga devotees. Some of us went to her show together and I was so impressed with her ceramic work that I bought one of her pieces to give to my yoga class. This inspired her to take me and another mutual friend to the Burren, the source of her inspiration. Here is a photo I took of the Burren.

The Burren in Western Ireland

It's incredibly beautiful in the Burren and I can see why my artist friend Noreen was inspired to make art from the images she saw there. She showed me the particular site which inspired her to create the framed ceramic piece I bought for the yoga class.

Here is a photograph I took of the arch that inspired Noreen's artwork

This is just one example of an Irish person who was kind to me. Another friend I made in yoga, Deirdre, invited me overnight to her house near Limerick and to her country home in West Cork. She knew one of my best American friends had taken her life while I lived in Ireland. As a result, I was planning to walk in a fundraiser for Pieta House, a group that provides free counseling for people affected by the suicide of loved ones. Deirdre got up with me at 3:30 in the morning and we drove together from her house to participate in the *Darkness into Light* annual 5 kilometer walk to raise funds for Pieta House. I felt strongly about this group since they helped me cope with the death of my dear friend through free counseling.

I could share more about other lovely Irish friends but I want to move on to Irish humor. Here is a photo I took of a T-shirt an Irish man was selling in the famous English Market in Cork.

One of the other funny signs I saw in Ireland was in a pub and it said, "I only drink on two occasions; When I'm thirsty and when I'm not." This quote is from Brendan Behan, an Irish poet.

The Irish love to laugh and they love their music too. I do as well. While in Ireland, I sang in the Limerick Choral Union and we performed several concerts of sacred works at the University of Limerick. I also traveled up to Armagh, in Northern Ireland, to do genealogical research about my mother's ancestors. While there, I got to sing with world renowned British composer John Rutter and about 200 other people in an Anglican church. That was a peak musical experience for me!

Remember I said I wanted to go to Ireland with my husband in part to reconnect with my mother by going back to places we had gone together. I still miss my mother terribly, even though she died 17 years ago. While in Armagh, I went back to the church steps where I had gone with her about 40 years earlier. Here is a photo of the two of us together on the same steps. The left hand photo of my lovely mother was taken by me while the photo on the right was taken by a kind stranger. This way, there is now one photo of us there together, if only in spirit.

My mother and me in the same place, separated only by time.

Life lesson: Irish people are lovely. If you ever have a chance to visit Ireland, please take it. You won't regret it. They are a kind, funny and music-loving people. But make sure to bring your umbrella or raincoat because it rains a real lot there. Notice how my mother and I are both holding onto raincoats in the photo?

Don't Judge a Book by its Cover
By Andrea Peers

"Appearances are often deceiving." –Aesop, a Greek storyteller famous for his fables

Appearances can be deceptive, we know. Think of trompe-l'oeil artwork which deceives the viewer into seeing a 3-D image, especially those incredible street artists who create an image with coloured sand, so realistic that you're astonished when they take a brush and sweep it away. No harm done, just a bit of light-hearted entertainment.

When meeting people for the first time, many of us make an initial assessment of them, based on their appearance and general demeanour. When we get to know them, we could decide that our first instinct was right or we might revise our opinion.

If the relationship is to be ongoing, such as with a new colleague or neighbour, it's usually wise to let things develop gradually. I'm reminded of the friendship between two of our neighbours in Spain. They moved in next door to each other in the same week and had an immediate rapport. Within days they were having breakfast together on one or the other's front porch. They enjoyed being able to speak their native tongue together. They were both German: but it turned out that was all they had in common. Within a year the bosom pals were not even speaking to each other.

Often we don't have the luxury of time to get to know someone before forming an opinion. In the 1970s my husband Mark and a friend decided to open a jazz club to showcase the bands they liked. They found a pub with a function room, booked up a list of regional bands, advertised in the local papers and heaved a sigh of relief when the opening night was a resounding success. These provincial band members all had day jobs but played for the love of music and some only charged expenses plus beer money. We charged admission at the door, in the hopes of covering their fee. Over time, the phrase 'swings and roundabouts' was used a lot. The nights when we made more than the fee put a bit in the kitty to pay for those when we didn't.

The club went from strength to strength, gaining a reputation for its variety and great atmosphere. Mark widened his horizons, booking well known professional bands from further afield. They cost a lot more but the risk usually paid off. Eventually as the membership grew, we moved to bigger premises and took bigger risks with some famous international musicians, some from as far away as America. From band fees in the hundreds of pounds they moved into the thousands and consequently there was more pressure to make sure no one slipped in without paying. After all, we would have to make up any short fall.

I must confess I was never really a jazz fan and was happy to sit at the door taking the entrance money. That way I got to know our regular members quite well. I also got to know the regular band members who would play our venue every few months in rotation, but it wasn't a problem if I didn't recognise one of them. Anyone carrying an instrument got past my eagle eye without challenge.

One night we had a professional band I knew from previous visits, with the addition of a famous guest soloist. As usual they all arrived together, in a jumble of bodies and instruments before the doors opened to the public and I barely glanced at them, except to say hello as they rushed past me.

During the half time interval people were milling around and I was chatting with some of the regulars. I noticed a scruffy, shifty looking individual, with lank greasy hair and a slouching posture, mooching around nearby. He sidled up to my table where I had tickets and cash. I interrupted my conversation to look up at him. He gestured towards my open packet of cigarettes and asked if he could have one. I refused quite abruptly and he moved away.

Imagine my horror when I learned that he was the star guest of the night; his name, which meant nothing to me, drawing in a full house of fans. He must have been mooching in search of a cigarette machine. One of our regulars was a journalist who waxed lyrical in his column the following week about the purity of sound and eloquence of his playing. He called it a memorable night. It certainly was for me. I'd made a quick judgement about a person that night, based on appearance alone.

Many years later our teenage daughter was robbed under our noses on the London Underground during rush hour. The four of us were slightly separated by the crowd but within sight of each other. I was sitting, my daughter standing near me. There was a disturbance when more people got into the already crowded carriage. A big athletic-looking black man shoved his way in, bashing his enormous sports bag into a neatly dressed middle aged white woman, who stumbled against my daughter but soon regained her balance. Several people asked if she was ok and criticised the man, who got off at the next stop, after throwing a few insults around. A seat became vacant next to me and the woman took it, staying on for one more stop.

Everyone who saw the incident judged the man as a lout and the woman as a victim, so different in appearance no one imagined they were connected. When we got off my daughter discovered all the zips on her bag were open and her purse was missing.

Only then did I recall an exchange between the man and the woman that struck a jarring note. He had responded rudely to the criticisms from other passengers and made some remark to the woman. It wasn't what she said in reply to him, but the inflection in her words that implied she knew him. The man created a diversion that distracted attention away from her but her respectable appearance and quiet demeanour fooled us all.

We all know conmen use their skills to trick people, dressing in a non-threatening style and cleverly adopting a trustworthy manner. With age we lose naivete and gain cynicism – or with luck we might end up somewhere between, experience honing our instincts. Whether we like it or not we judge and are judged on appearance. People have even been known to fall in love across a crowded room. What we wear says a lot about us and it is the first impression a stranger will have of us.

But demeanour is another important factor. If you saw a tramp dozing on a park bench with his little dog lying quietly beside him and a well-dressed person weaving around unsteadily with a bottle in their hand, which one would you most want to avoid? Experience teaches you to look beyond first impressions and not to judge the book by its cover.

Life Lesson: Don't make assumptions about people based on their appearance alone.

Famous Ancestors Can Inspire You
By Nancy Blodgett Klein

"No self is of itself alone. It has a long chain of intellectual ancestors. The "I" is chained to ancestry by many factors... This is not mere allegory, but an eternal memory."

— Erwin Schrödinger, an Austrian-Irish physicist

I have been a fan of genealogy for many years now, especially since my mother and father passed away. Studying my ancestry was a way I could feel more connected to them and to their histories. One of the interesting things I discovered while tracing my family line is that I am a fifth cousin to Harriet Beecher Stowe, the famous author of *Uncle Tom's Cabin*. Even though I am five generations removed from being her cousin, the shared heritage is still there. Henry David Thoreau is my sixth cousin, also five generations removed. He is the famous author of *Walden* and other well-known works. US President Ulysses Grant is my fifth cousin five generations removed while US President Franklin Delano Roosevelt was my sixth cousin, only four generations removed. Grant was an author too and finished his personal memoirs shortly before he died. President Roosevelt also published many books, though none of them were bestsellers.

So when I feel a compulsion to write a blog post, a magazine article or a book, I wonder if that is partly because the blood of other authors runs through my veins. One wonders whether shared DNA can also mean shared destiny.

Of course, being related to these four amazing people isn't much of an accomplishment by itself. It's more luck of the draw, not something I did but something I inherited upon my birth because of the ancestry of my mother's father, Charles William Deland. His surname used to be Delano or De Lannoy from near Lille, France, but it was changed to Deland after several generations of ancestors lived in America. Because of the Delano connection, Grant, FDR and Thoreau are all related to each other and to me. Harriet Beecher Stowe hooked into the Deland line more recently, about the same time period as she was living.

What I admire about these four ancestors isn't just that they were published authors and well-known public figures but that they all were honorable characters. Who they were *as people* is what attracts me about them. So let's review the positive traits that stand out among these four in order of their birth.

Harriet Beecher Stowe was born on June 14, 1811. One of the character traits she was known for was her integrity. She opposed slavery and used her intellect to write and publish a book opposing this unjust practice, at a time when many other White people were fine with it. She was brave, and not afraid to speak truth to power. This was all the more remarkable because when she published the anti-slavery book *Uncle Tom's Cabin* in 1851, women authors were not common. This made her doubly brave, to both highlight the cruelty of slavery when many Southerners, in particular, supported the practice and to speak out publicly as a woman author. The publication of her book helped open the eyes of more White people, turning many against the institution of slavery.

Henry David Thoreau was born July 12, 1817. He was an individualist, who was unafraid to confront others on behalf of his principles. He refused to pay a poll tax and spent a night in jail as a result. He used this time in jail to write a now-famous essay on civil disobedience. This essay argues for disobedience to law when the state is unjust in its actions, such as when it allows the cruel and unjust practice of slavery. To write and publish such an essay took a lot of courage, just as Beecher Stowe showed courage for publishing her book when she did. They were both abolitionists.

Thoreau is also famous for his book *Walden,* where he decided to live simply and alone out in the woods. Why did he do this? He explained in *Walden*:

"I went to the woods because I wished to live deliberately, to front only the essential facts of life, and see if I could not learn what it had to teach, and not, when I came to die, discover that I had not lived. I did not wish to live what was not life, living is so dear; nor did I wish to practice resignation, unless it was quite necessary. I wanted to live deep and suck out all the marrow of life, to live so sturdily and Spartan-like as to put to rout all that was not life, to cut a broad swath and shave close, to drive life into a corner, and reduce it to its lowest terms..."

This part of this book made such a great impression on me when I read it in high school that I decided to major in philosophy in college. This would allow me to read more books of such wisdom and depth, more books that were searching for life's meaning.

Ulysses S. Grant was born April 27, 1822. As General Grant, he showed great courage in leading the Union in battles to end the Civil War and keep the country united. He was a humble man who didn't put on airs and treated everyone with respect. Grant was also an honest man, although when he was President others around him were not as honest. His trust in the goodwill of other people hurt him both politically and financially.

As president, Grant worked hard to bring about reconciliation between the North and the South after the Civil War was over. The 15th Amendment was passed under the Grant Administration, giving Black men the right to vote. Grant also tried to limit activities of groups like the Ku Klux Klan that used violence to intimidate Black people and prevent them from voting.

Franklin Delano Roosevelt (FDR) was born January 30, 1882. He was a man of principle and action. He was a man of courage, as in, "We have nothing to fear but fear itself." Roosevelt had the leadership skills to guide the US through the Great Depression and most of World War II. He also recognized that without help from the US, Britain might lose WWII and Hitler could then control all of Europe. So FDR did what he could to help British Prime Minister Winston Churchill and the United Kingdom until he could bring the American public on board to directly support the Allies in the war.

So what do all of these ancestors have in common? They were all people of integrity and principle. For example, three of them opposed slavery and sought to end it in their own ways. They were all courageous and willing to take a stand even at their own expense. They all understood that every person has worth and dignity, not just some people.

I aspire to be like all of them in the way I live my life. Thank you, ancestors, for showing me how it's done. I pray I can live up to the examples you have set, in both word and deed, all the days of my life. May my life and writing be a tribute to you. God bless you, dear cousins.

Life Lesson: You are a product of all the ancestors who came before you. Make the most of yourself and your life and seek inspiration from your own ancestors who made a difference in the world, whether they were famous or not.

Be Grateful for Little Things, Especially When Life Isn't Going Well
By Nancy Blodgett Klein

"If you concentrate on finding whatever is good in every situation, you will discover that your life will suddenly be filled with gratitude, a feeling that nurtures the soul." — Rabbi Harold Kushner

Have you ever had a day where everything is going along great and then, all of a sudden, you wind up in an ambulance on your way to the hospital? Well, that happened to me Tuesday, March 30, 2021. I was attending an English immersion program, working as a volunteer to help Spanish people improve their English. We were at a hotel in Mengibar, in the old part of town, where public sidewalks and private pavements can be uneven.

I had left the hotel at the coffee break in search of cloth masks to wear as required during this awful pandemic. I had brought two pretty cloth masks with me but both had disappeared over the course of the five-day conference. Once outside the hotel, I started to search around for a pharmacy. Unfortunately, at that very moment, the sidewalk had gone from a flat surface to a steep step downwards, without any ramp or gradation. I put my left foot out into the air and landed on the ground with my left leg turning at a sickly right degree angle. I also heard my bone break.

Once down on the ground, I called out to a nearby young man with a red sweater to "Llame una ambulancia." He was kind and took off his sweater, putting it under my head to give me support. He asked me my name and, luckily, I was thinking clearly and gave him my lanyard with name badge that conference attendees wore during the event. He went inside the hotel and brought out the kind 40-something-year-old man who was in charge of the conference. We waited together for the ambulance to come. It was extremely hard going as I was in a lot of pain. After about 10 minutes, an ambulance arrived and the medical workers slowly and carefully got me into this white medical van for the 15 minute drive to the Neuro-Traumatologico Hospital in the mountainous Spanish city of Jaen, in Andalucía.

Thankfully, the conference leader was with me for all of this, both on the ambulance ride and in the emergency room. I was grateful for his companionship. Upon arrival, the medical staff decided I needed to have a Covid test so I got Q-tip-like objects stuck up both nostrils before anything else happened. This was definitely a prime example of adding insult to injury! I received a text message that night that my test result was negative.

The conference leader had kindly gone out and bought me an I-Phone charger at a nearby business so I could continue to use my phone while in the hospital. Having my phone was my lifeline to my family and friends.

After I left the emergency room, I was X-rayed. It was discovered I had broken my femur, the longest bone in one's body, in two places! After this painful procedure was done, I was transported to my room. Now I was truly alone and decided this was a really good time to cry. I did this without hesitation. Many tears were shed.

My husband couldn't join me at the hospital as he was four hours away in Orihuela Costa, in Alicante province, taking care of our cat and dog. Also, travel between provinces was not allowed and our car was still in the hotel parking lot in Mengibar.

Later that evening, medical staff wrapped my left leg in gauze and attached a rope to my ankle with a big weight at its end to help realign the leg. Two mornings later, a surgeon was available to do my operation. While waiting for my surgery, I got to enjoy the beautiful mountain ranges around Jaen. As a flatlander from Chicago, seeing mountains always gives me a thrill!

When they wheeled me down to surgery Thursday morning, I took the opportunity to ask the surgeon in Spanish if he had a lot of experience doing this kind of procedure. He replied that he was 44 years old and had been doing this operation for 20 years. Okay. We are good to go, I thought! This was great news and the exact type of thing to be grateful for during such an awful experience: I was in capable hands.

After about 3 hours of surgery (so I was told since I was out for the whole event), I woke up and promptly threw up. I only had enough time to say to the medical team, "Voy a vomiter," and voila, it happened.

I always had to speak Spanish during this ordeal as no one admitted to speaking more than a few words of English. Here are some new words I learned in my own hospital-based Spanish immersion program! Cuña is bedpan, pañal is diaper, muletas are crutches, manta is blanket, pastilla para dormir is sleeping pill and timbre is bell (to call the nurses). This last one is key!

Here are some Spanish phrases I learned: To tell the nurse that my bell, my pills and my charger cord fell down, you need to say, "Mi timbre, mis pastillas y el cable del cargador se cayeron." If you want the nurse to open the window, you need to say, "Puedes abrir la ventana?" If you want your IV off, you say, ¿Puedes quitarlo?" This whole experience helped me improve my intermediate-level Spanish. So that was undoubtedly a blessing!

Once my surgery was over and I was wheeled into recovery, I discovered I was the only patient in a post-op room normally as busy as a train station. The two nurses there said the room typically had 20 to 25 people in it. It turns out that this was the day before Good Friday, though, so only emergency surgeries were taking place. I was lucky to have been operated on when I was. Semana Santa is a big deal in Spain so things really slow down Easter weekend. This was something to be grateful for after such a traumatic injury.

Once back to my hospital room Thursday night, I was glad to have the operation behind me. The next day was Good Friday. Nobody came by to help me start walking again, as one doctor had led me to believe might happen.

Both Friday and Saturday were days of resting in bed and replying to the many messages of sympathy and support I was receiving from family and friends via What's App, text message, email and Facebook Instant Messenger. I had never felt so supported by so many people in my entire life! This was another blessing during a dark ordeal. For example, our older son Alex called me three nights in a row from California and this was something that had never happened before. I was feeling the love.

Finally, on Easter Sunday, one nurse let me use a walker with a plastic seat to move around my room. "Nancy Klein is risen today. Al-le-lu-i-a!" I was never so happy in all my life to be able to use the toilet. This is something we take for granted in normal times, of course. But after five days of using bedpans, I mean cuñas, I was thrilled to use a toilet. Plus, I could never bring myself to have a bowel movement in the bedpan so using the toilet after five days lapse was a major blessing! Also on Easter, I received the best meal of my stay. It included roast pork, green peppers, paella and fresh peaches. This was something else to be grateful for.

The next day, I thought my physical therapy would begin. Instead, the doctor who operated on me came in my room and said I could go home! Lord have mercy, was I excited! This was the best blessing of all. Unfortunately, it cost me $600 to take a four-hour cab ride home because my medical insurance company wouldn't pay for my transport. Nonetheless, I got to sleep in my own bed that night with our ginger cat purring by my side. That experience was priceless!

Life Lesson: When things go horribly wrong, try to focus on what you can be grateful for, rather than wallowing in your misery.

Don't Play Favourites with Your Children
By Brenda Darling

"The sun and moon shine on all without partiality." —*Confucius*

I was the third of four children although I believe that I must have been invisible as I was always put to one side, left to make my own devises. I had food, I never starved, and when needs be I had clothes, hand-me-downs from my older brother, like vests and socks, even old worn-out shoes and coats. My mother went to work and left my dad to do whatever needed to be done, like cooking. After my much older sister got married and moved away, I became the cleaner.

My older sister was 14 years older than I was. She had told me that mother always made her feel like a burden, as all she ever wanted was a boy. It was the same situation for me. So, as I grew up, I had no choice but to accept the lack of affection I got from her. But I could not help noticing that she always found time for my older brother and younger sister. Favourite was a word that my brother insisted on saying whenever I had to clear up after him. Yes, she loved him, and she loved her baby, her last child, my sister, and she never stopped letting me know where I came in the pecking order. Favourite, my brother, followed by my young sister, then my dad, and I was last. My older sister was long gone.

Two of my siblings were showered with love and money, nothing was too good for them. Whereas I had to be thankful for all that I had received. In my innocence, I just got on with it, tried to get a spark, a tender touch, a loving kiss, from my mother, but no, her time was taken up pampering the others. She either never noticed my unhappiness, or she just never cared.

I have tried hard to remember if I had ever been shown love but if so, why can't I remember images of places of when I felt wanted? Throughout her life, mother never changed. Even when it came to grandchildren, she had her favourites, and it wasn't my children. I never asked to be born, and yet I still loved my mother. She gave me life and with all her faults I believe that she had taught me a good lesson without meaning too. That is, love without condition, spread your love around and never have favourites as it scars and never heals. Her lack of feelings and tenderness made me strong, without even knowing it.

When I became a Mum, my heart ached with happiness for the first time in my life. To kiss and hug my children and grandchildren is the best feeling in the world. I reminded them that I loved them all, each and every day and that they should always love each other even if they have faults, as nobody is perfect. I believe that I taught them tolerance and forgiveness and that showing your love is not a weakness.

Now I feel like I am an incredibly lucky woman because I have four wonderful children who have grown into strong, yet soft-hearted human beings who make me proud every day. You would have thought that my mother, being second to last in a family of seven children, and brought up having to share her parents' affection, would have cherished all her own children. Sometimes I wonder if her parents had favourites too, and she was just carrying on where they left off? In any case, she was my mother, not my mum.

My promise to my children throughout their lives was that I was their parent first but also a friend. When I raised them, I admit to having stalked them at times, shouted at them, lectured them, driven them insane and been their worst nightmare. At times, I hunted them down like a bloodhound because that is what a mum does to show her love. You will never find someone who loved, prayed, cared and worried more about their children more than I did. If they hadn't hated me once in their lives, then have not done my job properly!

Life Lesson: If you have children or grandchildren, love them all equally and don't play favourites. It's very damaging to a child's self-esteem to feel like they aren't loved as much as their siblings. Such favouritism can cause anger and depression that may not go away when these children become adults themselves.

A Loving Relationship Can Make Life's Last Stages More Enjoyable

By Anthony Jones

"And in the end, the love you take is equal to the love you make."
—Paul McCartney

I wake up from a temporary oblivion that could have been twenty minutes or two seconds, such is the depth of the mental blackout from which I have just emerged. Where am I? Sitting in the driver's seat of my car at a set of traffic lights that are still mercifully red. Where? Sainsbury's on my right... yes, I'm in Leytonstone High Road, on my way to spend an hour with Mr. Jack, my fifth call of the day, vacuum his flat and sort out his shopping at... Sainsbury's of course! Now it all makes sense. Body and mind re-engage – feet to pedals, hands to wheel and brain focussed on the objectives ahead, Mr. Jack, always a pleasant hour, and then – oh, God! – Mr. Choudri.

I have been a care worker for three months and have discovered a different world from the one I have inhabited for the first thirty odd years of my working life. I race from one client to another, as many as eight calls a day, bathing, feeding, cleaning and shopping for the elderly and the disabled: splendid and rewarding work, though sadly on an hourly rate at minimum wage, and paying for my own fuel. If my car is laid up, then so am I. The company with whom I hold this tenuous employment boast a huge logo on the wall of their reception proclaiming their right to be known as 'Investors in People.' The extent of their investment in my case is a day's course in handling lifting equipment, a company shirt and a box of surgical gloves.

My 'parish' covers the North London borough of Waltham Forest which runs from the leafy prosperity of Chingford on the Northern boundary of London, Southwards to the inner-city squalor of Leytonstone – the fictional Walford of BBCs *East Enders* - a concrete purgatory inhabited by a population who have long abandoned any hope of salvation. And as the geography unfolds, so does the class and status of the clientele I serve, and beyond that the individual circumstances of those clients and the long and varied histories they carry with them.

Mr. Hall is my first call. A sharp-featured, hunched man in his mid-sixties, he lives in a smart block of private flats overlooking the local golf course, with the green fields of Epping leading to the horizon. He came to London from Bristol many years ago to make his money in shipping. He is plainly comfortably off in his well-ordered home, but the grotesquely emaciated body that reveals itself when he removes his silk dressing gown tells the full sad tale of a man who has everything and nothing. I help him with his shower, apply emollient to his anus - Shakespeare's *Seven Ages of Man* running through the back of my mind - prepare his breakfast of tea and toast, clear up and leave for my next call. In the normal order of existence life is seldom cruel in the real sense, but its randomness can make it seem that way. Mr. Harmer is in the last of the seven ages of man and will be dead in another four months.

Mr. Wood is my second call. A tall, gentle man who used to be the headmaster of the local secondary school, his health is in sharp decline. He is Anglo-Welsh and a sports fanatic, but age has finally enfeebled his impressive frame and his mind is becoming clouded. The news of the English cricket team's progress in Australia sets the tenor of his day. If the Aussies are on the back foot he is spry and brisk; an English batting collapse (often the case!) will leave him having to be helped out of bed, his enthusiasm for the day already destroyed.

Through all this he is propped up by his petite wife. Calm, gentle and resolute, her blend of toughness and love are inspiring. I think to myself then that however grim life may get, love truly does have the power to drive back the shadows. The pair of them remind me so much of my own parents at the same stage of their lives. I help Mr. Wood with his ablutions, dress him, sort out the laundry if it's been a bad night, and then on to the next call.

Mr. Williams lives in a private care home, is in his early eighties and suffers from depression. Most of his memories centre around the War, when he served in a tank regiment and was in Germany at the final surrender. He was wounded twice; once in the face by an itinerant in the chaos that followed surrender and previously to that in the backside. "There was no toilet in the tank, you had to leave it if you needed a shit – and that's when the bastards would be waiting for you!" he exclaims with some venom.

He did not enjoy a happy marriage and is convinced that his third and youngest son is the product of an affair his wife had with a German POW. This is the son who looks after him and visits him regularly, an irony apparently lost on Mr. Williams. He is lucky to have a loved one paying attention to him. This is not the case for many of my patients.

Next stop is Mr. Affleck. He escaped to London in the Swinging Sixties, taking the road travelled by so many Scots over the centuries. His heart is definitely not in the Highlands. A tall, handsome man who has not lost the soft Highland lilt that marks his country of origin, he must have lived a life style uncountenanced in those mist shrouded hills, but along the way he has paid the price and now suffers from cerebral syphilis. His physical movement is restricted to the extent of being almost completely housebound. No shower here, but a proper bath, breakfast and dressing. In fact, in his prime, Mr. Affleck was a theatrical dresser and worked on the hugely successful drama series *Upstairs Downstairs*. He remembers Gordon Jackson as a very fussy person, "Everything had to be just so with him," he recalls.

Mr. Affleck is a hoarder. His terrace house has at least two entire rooms stuffed to the rafters with furniture of all kinds, Bakelite radios, vintage electronics, framed pictures, tools, box files and walls of VHS video cassettes. Do they hold memories for him or are they simply random purchases that never quite found a proper use? His brother and sister-in-law visit every other year, although he seems pretty dismissive of their attention. In a strange way he seems content.

My next patient is Mr. Kurcskyi, who won't ever be going back to the Ukraine. He slipped out of the USSR in the chaos of WWII and ended the war as an interpreter for the British 8th Army in Italy. How on earth did he end up in Italy? "You had to be quick on your feet," he replies with a sly twinkle. He found asylum in Britain, married an English girl and has an attentive daughter, who pays him regular visits in his care home accommodation. Mr. Kurckyi resembles a hobbit, small and wrinkled, his dingy apartment a hobbit hole, but what a life he led; from Stalin's Russia, the famines and the purges, through the Nazi onslaught, through the war in Italy, to the rest of his life, spent in a foreign country with a different culture, history and language, his homeland a closed door for fifty years. Does he ever miss pre-war Ukraine? I suspect not. A monochrome photo on his sideboard shows him downing pints with his workmates at Longbridge. His smile is one of a survivor.

There are others such as Mr. O'Connor, a legless diabetic from Walthamstow who serenaded me with Fifties showstoppers as I shaved him and prepared his breakfast. His *Joie de Vivre* was a tonic. There is Mr. Akar, a terminal addict to nicotine who was smoking himself to death in front of his distressed family while attached to an industrial-sized nebulizer. I got on very well with him, his self-destruction notwithstanding, and his wife cooked me a glorious lunch of stuffed vine leaves.

Finally, there is Mr. Choudri. Always the last call, the final challenge in a long day, in Leytonstone - London's heart of darkness. As I park outside his terrace house I can see a burning car halfway down the block. It is unattended, its destruction uncelebrated, unremarked, unmourned. I leave it to burn and ring the bell. A pause and then a bellowed response – "I'm coming you fucking bastaaard!" The door opens and Choudri's half- paralysed frame stands before me, dripping black smudges around his temples where he has been attempting to dye his hair. "Sorry, gentleman," he says, "come in."

Mr. Choudri was a successful businessman and was responsible for one of East London's biggest 'chicken and rib' food outlets before a severe stroke crippled his body. How much it has done to his mind as well is uncertain. Some of his decision making is okay, some of it simply delusional. I attempt to plot a course between the two. Choudri's sons look after the business now, but not their father - he is not on good terms with them. "My son has a big bushy beard," he told me after a recent filial visit, "like a bush, and you know what you find in a bush? A SNAKE!" Rapprochement was obviously off the agenda on that occasion.

Apart from his dysfunctional aggression, the most memorable and terrible thing about Mr. Choudri is the utter squalor in which he exists. His two-up two-down terrace house is a filthy, unkept shambles, a smell of urine hanging in the air. Dead mice are not uncommon, leaving one to speculate on the number of live ones. This is one stop above all others where I appreciated the surgical gloves.

Choudri is a Pakistani and a devout Muslim who can still hobble the distance to the local mosque. The mosque does not appear to give much back, but Mr. C's manners probably have something to do with that. I was present at a meeting where the improvement of Choudri's wretched lot was discussed. The team included an impressively on-the-ball young Asian who went out of his way to be helpful. Mr. Choudri appeared receptive at the time, and I remarked afterwards on the young man's efforts on his behalf – "F##king Bangladeshi!" came the retort, "We carry them! We carry them!"

Mr. Choudri is later moved into care. He was an unhappy man who was stingy with love and affection. No surprise then that he was alone at the end.

Life Lesson: At the last stage of life, it's better to have loving care from a significant other or family member than from a minimum wage employee run so ragged that they are falling asleep at the wheel. Until then, remember to be a kind person who doesn't

push loved ones away by bad behaviour or you are more likely to end up alone.